Aquarium
Guide

Back to Nature

AQUARIUM GUIDE

Kjell Fohrman

ISBN 0-9668255-2-7

Cichlid Press
P.O. Box 13608
El Paso, TX 79913
www.cichlidpress.com

Contents

Photos cover, p. 1, and p. 4 by Michael Prasuhn.
Photo p. 3 by Kjell Fohrman.

Preface

There are few pieces of furniture that can compete with an aquarium as regards beauty. The appearance of the aquarium is a matter of personal taste, but one thing is for sure: there is an aquarium to suit everybody! An aquarium beautifully decorated with plants and a large shoal with cardinal tetras, an aquarium with rocks and brightly-coloured Malawi cichlids, an aquarium with magnificent discus and peaceful catfishes — there is something for every taste. An aquarium is not only a piece of furniture but also a piece of nature brought into the living room. There is always something going on in the tank — some fishes may spawn, some may fight, some may die. These things are all natural processes that can teach a lot to children and adults alike.

Setting up an aquarium means, among other things, assuming the responsibility of providing the fishes with the right environment so that they will be happy and healthy, but this is not always easy. Over the years I have started up more than a thousand aquaria and have learned that there are no two tanks the same. Like all other aquarists I have gone through four stages:

1/ The beginner stage — you don't know a lot but are eager to learn.

2/ The "expert" stage — you think you know everything (you have read one book and have an aquarium that works perfectly until ...).

3/ The beginner stage part two - (algae takes over the aquarium, the fish get sick and die) A stage that every aquarist has to go through to some degree; you realise that the perfect aquarium is largely an illusion.

4/ The aquarist — who has learned that the biological balance that he or she has tried to create in the aquarium may get disturbed

Kjell Fohrman

— even though he or she has done everything right. Such a hobbyist is continually learning, but may even so still suffer temporary setbacks (but not as often as in the past). A true aquarist will gradually develop "wet fingers" (the equivalent of a gardener's green fingers), i.e. he or she develops an instinctive feeling for what is right for the aquarium. The aquarist learns to spot whether a fish is falling sick or if the aquarium water is getting out of balance, etc.

There is no golden rule for aquaria, nothing to say that if you do things in a particular way success is always guaranteed. On the contrary, there are a lot of different ways to reach your goal: a beautiful and interesting aquarium. In this small introduction to the aquarium hobby, I have described the way that has worked for me, and I will try to give some hints and advice. I would, however, recommend that you acquire further knowledge by reading other books as well, subscribing to an aquarium magazine, joining a (local) aquarium club, and visiting a number of good aquarium stores.

This book is based on my own 25 years of experience in the aquarium business. What I have learned over the years is, as is often the case, to a great extent based on the knowledge passed on to me by other aquarists. I have read their books and articles in aquarium magazines, listened to their lectures, and talked with them at aquarium club meetings. If, by writing this book, I can pass some knowledge to you, the reader, then I am most certainly happy to do so. However, do not regard this book as a definitive guide to success with your aquarium. On the contrary, read it critically and apply its advice to your own specific situation, in order to make your aquarium exactly the way you want it.

This is no more than a basic general book on tropical aquarium fishes; if you wish to specialise in a particular direction then you should also acquire any other relevant titles in the Back to Nature series, or other books that apply to the fishes you wish to keep or the aquarium you want to create.

Finally I would like to express my gratitude to several aquarists who have made it possible for me to write this book. For example, the book contains very few photos that are mine, Mark Smith, Ad Konings and Ole Pedersen took the majorities, but other aquarists have contributed as well. Thanks to all these people for their beautiful photos. I am very grateful for help from Lasse Forsberg, Claus Christensen, Mary Bailey and in particular from my wife Hjördis, who all have read parts of the text and, of course, found some mistakes to correct. I hope that there are not too many left!

With aquaristic regards
Kjell Fohrman

The Aquarium

A short history

In Asia (primarily in China and Japan) there is a tradition of keeping fishes in tanks - just for the pleasure of watching them - which goes back several hundred years, with goldfish and carp the main focus of interest. The fishes were historically kept not in glass tanks, but in containers varying from simple earthenware vessels to special china ones.

Glass tanks are an invention of the western world and started to get popular in the middle of the 19th century. In the beginning they were rather exclusive and reserved for well-to-do aquarists. Those early aquaria were constructed by fixing panes of glass into a frame using putty. The first heating equipment was for example kerosene and alcohol light, which were placed beneath the aquarium.

Frame aquaria were far from safe, and leakage was quite common. Hence it was a great step

An example of an ordinary aquarium from 1930, in a mail order catalogue from the German company Scholze & Pötzschke.

forward when, in the sixties, silicone sealant was introduced as a bonding material for manufacturing "all-glass" aquaria. Thanks to silicone the aquarium hobby has developed tremendously during the last few decades, and the accompanying slump in prices has

A transport with aquaria from Scholze & Pötzschke in Berlin, Germany, to a public aquarium in Bergen, Norway.

brought a tank into most people's homes. A large number of innovations have been made in the field of filtration; there are efficient filter materials on the market, there are water conditioners to treat all kinds of water to meet the demand of different fishes; nutritious high quality foods have been developed; and so on. On top of all this, the supply of fishes has increased immensely, partly due to improved communications with remote parts of the globe, but mainly because a lot of fishes are being bred in captivity today — in particular in Asia but also in other parts of the world.

The shape of the aquarium

For many years the aquarium itself always looked much the same, i.e. it was a rectangular glass box. It is only in the last ten years that the design has started to change. Today there are corner aquaria, tanks with a slanting front glass and mansard corners, etc. Nowadays the aquarium, its support, and its cover are often integrated into a single piece of furniture. There are tanks that will fit into every home and suit every taste. Shape is simply a matter of personal preference.

The so-called goldfish bowl is not something that I would recommend, since it is far too small, which makes it impossible to achieve a biological balance.

The size of aquarium you choose

It's much more difficult to get a good balance in a small aquarium than it is in a larger one.

will depend, of course, on how much space you have available and what fishes are to be kept in it. In general it is true to say that it is far easier to maintain a stable balance in a larger aquarium. The larger the tank, the greater the safety factor against anything going seriously wrong. I would recommend an aquarium of at least 100-litre capacity, preferably 150-200 litres (or more).

A lot has happened in aquarium design. Here is a corner aquarium with slanted front panels and mansard corners, containing rainbow fishes.

Where should the aquarium be sited?

1. An aquarium is rather heavy (a 150-litre aquarium, fully decorated, weighs approx. 200 kg) and should therefore be placed on a stable base.

2. The aquarium should be sited where it cannot be affected by direct sunlight, since this can cause problems with algae.

3. It should also be sited where it is relatively quiet.

The Siamese fighting fish, *Betta splendens*, is a popular but aggressive aquarium-fish.

4. Close to an electrical power point and, if possible, a water supply (especially if it is a large aquarium).

5. It should be positioned so that it is easy to clean the filter, the glass, etc.

6. Remember that the flooring underneath and around the aquarium will be liable to spillage during maintenance.

7. The aquarium must be positioned level. Failure to do so is the most common cause of the glass breaking.

8. If the glass of the aquarium is not protected by a frame, you must place a thin (approx. 1 cm thick) sheet of Styrofoam between the aquarium and the base.

Making your own aquarium

Suppose you want to have an aquarium somewhere in your home where an "off the shelf" one will not fit. In that case you will have to make your own. This is not easy without previous experience. Before you start, I would recommend you get in touch with an aquarium club, where there will be experts. A leakage can be very expensive, and in some instances your household insurance may not cover the damage if you made the aquarium yourself. Ideally check first with your insurance company to see whether they have any special rules regarding aquaria.

When making a tank yourself you must also be careful when choosing the type of silicone. There are a lot of different qualities, and most of these are suitable only for small aquaria. The packaging should specify whether a particular type can be used for aquaria. Most silicone glues on the market are intended for bathrooms and contain fungicides, which are deadly to fish. The silicone sold in aquarium stores is, however, safe to use.

A jacuzzi, a bottle of champagne and an aquarium with Malawi cichlids, is a good way to enjoy life.

Interior decoration

A chapter about aquarium decor can be as large as one cares to make it. It is a subject so huge that it could fill the pages of quite a number of books. The kind of decoration you choose will depend on what you consider attractive, what size it is, the kind of fish that will be kept with it, and so on. Maybe you want to imitate a particular biotope. If you want to set up a biotope aquarium, I would recommend that you first read some of the other books that have been published in the Back to Nature series.

Here we will concentrate on rather general aspects. My personal starting points, when decorating an aquarium, are (1) try to imitate nature, (2) bring the aquarium in line with what is good for the fishes, and (3) make it beautiful to look at. Unfortunately most standard aquaria are hard to decorate since they are often higher than deeper; the other way around would be better from a decorating point of view.

a harmonious creation (for you as observer and for the fishes as occupants). Six years ago the so-called Back to Nature backgrounds were introduced on to the market, which was a giant leap forward for the aquarium hobby (judging by the many subsequent imitations). These backgrounds are exact replicas of a rock wall or a root. Nowadays there are many imitations of the Back to Nature backgrounds, but none comes close to the original. These backgrounds are placed inside the

The Back to Nature backgrounds are exact replicas of rock walls or roots.

aquarium and have both pros and cons. One advantage is that you can conceal a big filter and/or an immersion heater behind the background (it is hard to imagine something more unnatural and unattractive than a visible heater or filter in the aquarium). A disadvantage is that it somewhat reduces the swimming space available for the fishes.

If you do not want to spend that much money on a background, there are other possibilities, for

Background

The background in or behind the aquarium is essential in making the aquarium a beautiful sight and

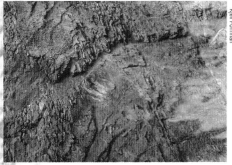

The best plastic pictorial backgrounds are those with single-coloured subjects like this.

instance painting the back glass a dark colour. Another alternative is to buy a commercially produced paper or plastic pictorial background. The best ones are those with single-coloured subjects, such as a rock. A background with plants or, even worse, one that depicts a coral reef, gives a much too confusing impression. But the decision is a matter of personal opinion — the fish could not care less!

Gravel

If the bottom is too light, the fish may become shy, so a fairly dark

Some fishes, like *Satanoperca leucosticta*, like to sift sand through the gills and therefore prefer a fine bottom substrate.

type of gravel is preferable. The grain size will depend on whether or not you want to have plants in your aquarium, and also on what kind of fishes you want to have. Some fishes like to sift gravel through their gills or simply pick in it to find edible particles. Examples of such fishes are some cichlid species (e.g. *Geophagus*) and a number of catfishes (e.g. *Corydoras*). These species prefer a grain size of maximum 2 mm. In a planted aquarium the gravel should not be coarser than 2 to 3 mm.

How thick the layer of gravel should be depends on whether the tank contains plants or not. In a planted aquarium it should be 6-10 cm, otherwise 3-6 cm will be fine. Some kinds of gravel contain calcium (e.g. crushed marble and coral gravel) which makes the water alkaline. This should be avoided in most cases (except where the water is extremely soft — see WATER). If in doubt you can check if the gravel contains calcium by dropping hydrochloric acid on it (or on the stones). If it foams or bubbles, it contains calcium. As you may not always have hydrochloric acid at hand, you can also use a lime-scale remover (as sold for coffee machines or tiles), or even just vinegar. The foaming effect is less visible with the weaker acids but it will still give you an indication.

Great care must be exercised when handling strong acids — wear rubber gloves and goggles, wash off splashes with plenty of

The guppy is a very adaptable fish and therefore goes well in most community aquaria.

All *Corydoras* (photo *Corydoras schwartzii*) need fine-grained gravel (max 2 mm). The gravel in this photo tank is normally too coarse for *Corydoras*.

since "fresh wood" may contain toxic substances. Most wood, however, contains tannic acid to some extent, and as this makes the water more acid you should avoid putting too much wood in any one aquarium, especially if it contains cichlids from lakes Malawi and Tanganyika or livebearers from Central America. You should never collect wood from the wild yourself — buy it in an aquarium store instead. In this case you can be pretty sure that it will not harm the fish. Do not buy too much, however. It may influence the pH value of the water and make the water look rather brown, in particular in the beginning.

Another problem with wood is that it will not sink initially. Soaking for a few weeks, weighing it down with rocks, is the easiest way

water, and seek medical help if necessary.

When you decorate an aquarium, you should always make sure that the gravel layer is deeper at the back of the aquarium and that it slopes downwards toward the front glass. You can achieve this most easily by building small terraces of stones or wood.

Wood

Wood can be very decorative in an aquarium and is sometimes mandatory, e.g. for some catfishes. All wooden materials must have been "dead" for quite some time,

to solve this problem. You should be careful in placing rocks on the wood though, as totally dry wood is full of air and thus has enormous buoyancy. If the "weights" fall off, the wood can destroy a lot on its way up to the surface.

Rocks

You can find a lot of beautiful rocks in an aquarium store, but you can also look for them in nature. Make sure, however, that you avoid limestone types of rock (if you do not have fish that enjoy alkaline water). Limestone and marble leach a considerable amount of calcium; lava, basalt, and granite do not contain calcium. Be careful with slates! Some types can contain oil or metal oxides that can leach into the aquarium water.

Do not mix different types of rocks in your aquarium, use one type (or no more than two different types which have some points of similarity). If you have a lot of rocks in your tank, you should also place a 1 cm thick sheet of Styrofoam on the bottom of the aquarium, under the gravel. The rocks must be built up from the bottom of the tank, i.e. they should not be placed on the gravel. The reason for this is that some fishes may dig and thus undermine a rock, with sometimes disastrous consequences. Therefore always place the rocks on the bottom of the aquarium before filling with gravel.

Other decor materials

Of course there are a lot of different materials that can be used when setting up an aquarium. In the autumn you can collect beech leaves from the ground (if they do not sink, put them in hot water for a short while). In addition, bamboo and other materials can be used.

The rocks must be built up from the bottom of the tank, otherwise fish may undermine the setup, with sometimes disastrous results.

I have deliberately not mentioned divers, treasure chests, skeletons, and so on. Once, when I was running an aquarium store, I decorated an aquarium with scarlet-coloured gravel, neon-coloured plastic plants, miniature divers,

14

Many South American catfishes, such as this *Scobiancistrus aureatus*, have become very popular among aquarists.

One of the most beautiful aquarium fishes is the Dwarf Gourami, *Colisa lalia*, which exists in several colour variants.

and treasure chests, etc. The fish population consisted of veil-tail goldfishes with bubble-eyes and gigantic fins. This was supposed to be an example of how not to decorate your aquarium. Unfortunately this test was a disaster, because everybody wanted to buy such a tank! I had to quickly remove it. As far as I am concerned, the aquarist should try to imitate the natural environment.

Accessories like the ones above do not harm the fish, but most aquarists would prefer the aesthetic pleasure of aquaria that imitate nature itself. But then again, tastes differ. I am pretty sure that there are people out there who would love to mix ice cream with ketchup. But even though the mixture is harmless to people, I would not consider it a good combination.

Water

Even though a certain water quality and chemistry might be acceptable for human beings, that does not necessarily mean that it is suitable to use in aquaria. Different fish species come from different habitats with different water conditions, ranging from the relatively acid waters of the rainforests in South America (with a pH below 7.0) to the alkaline waters of the great east African lakes (with a pH above 7.5); and fishes' requirements as regards water likewise vary from species to species. Many aquarium fishes, however, are highly adaptable, but it remains important that water parameters should be as consistent as possible, since fishes are sensitive to large and rapid changes in the pH value in particular.

The pH value is a measurement of the acidity and alkalinity of the water and is measured using a scale ranging from 0 to 14, with pH 7 representing neutral; above 7 is alkaline and below 7 is acid. The pH value will depend on whether any substances dissolved in the water — minerals, organic materials — are alkaline or acidic, and on the quantity of such substances present.

A further water important parameter which should be measured is its hardness, which is the measurement of the quantity of certain dissolved minerals (salts) present. Different types of water contain different kinds of dissolved calcium and magnesium salts, and the greater the quantity of these, the harder the water. In practice this is measured by testing the general or total hardness of the

These Tanganyika cichlids, *Cyphotilapia frontosa*, *Neolamprologus sexfasciatus* and *N. pulcher*, need alkaline water.

water (GH, measured in degrees — dGH) and or the carbonate hardness (KH, again measured in degrees — dKH). In the wild waters with a high hardness are nor-

Water with a pH between 6 and 7 provides good conditions for a planted aquarium with cardinal tetras (*Paraheirodon axelrodi*).

mally alkaline, while soft water (low hardness) is commonly neutral or acid. This does not necessarily mean, however, that tap water always follows this rule.

Tap water varies from city to city and from country to country. I live in a city where the tap water has a high pH value (around 8), and at the same time the water is soft (KH around 1). Soft water (KH of 3 or below) has a low buffering capacity, i.e. the lack of minerals means that the pH will be unstable, and may easily fall rapidly (within a couple of days), with serious consequences for the fish. The buffer capacity is not as directly important to the fish as the pH value, but a lack of it may thus have an indirect influence on the fishes.

These and some other water parameters can easily be meas-

ured using the various test kits on the market.

As I mentioned in the introduction to this chapter, different fishes have different requirements, even though they adapt fairly easy. Suitable pH-levels are specified when the fish species are discussed in the second part of this book.

Over the last few years several products have been developed that will create suitable values as regards water parameters. Everything from various liquids (e.g. oak extract) through reverse osmosis systems to peat pellets (buy a high quality type; the cheapest ones provide only a very small and short-term effect).

Below are some examples of how to adjust the water using different methods:

The Siamese fighting fish tolerates water with pH-levels varying between 6 and 8.

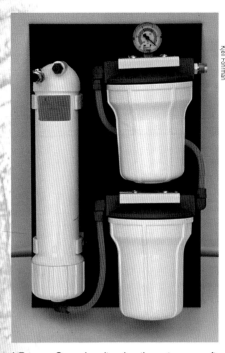

A Reverse Osmosis unit makes the water very soft.

To increase the carbonate hardness:

1. Use calcareous gravel (e.g. marble chips or coral gravel) as filter material .

2. Use water treatments from the aquarium store.

To decrease the hardness:

1. Add reverse osmosis water mixed with tap water (not pure reverse osmosis water).

2. Use water treatments from the aquarium store.

To decrease the pH-value:

1. If the water is not very soft — add CO_2 (carbon dioxide), using a regulated supply.

2. Peat filtration (most effective with soft water).

3. Use a water treatment from the aquarium store (e.g. oak extract).

To increase the pH-value.

1. Add sodium bicarbonate (can be bought in the grocery store as baking soda).

2. Powerful circulation of the aquarium — to dispel supersaturated levels of dissolved carbon dioxide into the atmosphere — can sometimes raise the pH. The effectiveness of this procedure will depend on the amount of waste products in the aquarium.

3. Use water treatments from the aquarium store.

N.B. **never increase the pH-value without first performing a partial water change**.

If you raise the pH, ammonium ions in the water will covert to toxic ammonia. By making a partial water change you will dilute the amount of ammonium.

If you use different treatments to adjust the water parameters, make sure you always check the effect on pH by measuring the latter with

Even if most plants prefer soft, slightly acid water, a number of them, such as this *Nymphea lotus* (red form), grows well in all kinds of water.

a pH-test kit every now and then until the value is stabilized.

Water conditioners

In a lot of cities the tap water contains chlorine (chlorine gas, chlorine dioxide) that may harm the mucus coating and gill tissue of the fish. The bulk of the chlorine can be eliminated when performing a partial water change by filling up with new water under high pressure (e.g. through a shower head) causing the gas to be driven off into the atmosphere. Unfortunately some water companies (check with you local company) add not only chlorine gas/chlorine dioxide but also ammonium sulphate, combined to form chloramine, which is impossible to get rid of mechanically and can be deadly to fishes, even in small doses. If your local water company uses choramine you must use a dechlorinating water conditioner, and no more than 20 % of the water should be changed every week.

Water conditioners can be used to get rid of chlorine/chloramine and some metals in the tap water, and sometimes contain substances to protect the mucous coating of the fishes. You should always use water conditioners when you start up an aquarium and when you perform a large partial water change. But when you make normal partial water changes it is not always necessary to use water conditioners.

When starting up an aquarium you should buy only a small number of fishes, since there is no useful and vital bacterial culture present yet. Step by step you can add some more fishes. During the first month you should feed very carefully, since it takes approxi-

The platy (*Xiphophorus maculatus*) is one of the most popular aquarium fishes, mainly because it is beautiful but also because it is a hardy fish.

Dermogenys pusillus is not a fish for the beginner since it is aggressive, sensitive, needs live food and prefers brackish water.

mately one month to establish the right balance in the aquarium. If you do not follow this rule, you will get nitrite (a product of the nitrogen cycle, the break down of waste products) in the aquarium and all the fish may die.

You can speed up the establishment of a good bacteria population by adding a special bacteria culture that can be bought from the aquarium store. Another almost as effective method is to take a handful of gravel from an already-established aquarium when starting up a new aquarium (the gravel must not be cleaned). Another good method is to transfer some filter medium from an established filter to the new one.

1. Keep a small number of fishes during the first month (more if you add bacterial culture).
2. Feed the fish sparingly (especially during the first month).
3. Do not increase the "loading" of the aquarium rapidly (i.e. do not add too many fish at the same time).
4. Add a bacteria culture.

How to get rid of nitrite:
1. Change water — but when you change water, add water from another aquarium — not tap water.
2. Add a bacteria culture.
3. Add some marine or rock salt (reduces the detrimental effects of the nitrite but does not get rid of it).
4. Change water using tap water — using tap water can make things worse since beneficial bacteria attached to small particles in the water may be lost with the old water. If you change using tap water, then change only a small amount (max. 5 %) several times

a day and only in combination with using a bacteria culture.

Tests

As can be seen from the above, you will need some basic types kinds of water test kits, and these can all be bought in aquarium stores. When you set up your aquarium you should have at least the following types: pH, KH, NO_2 (nitrite).

Test the water frequently in the beginning; after about a month once a week will be sufficient.

In this book I have tried merely to suggest simple ways of dealing with different kinds of problems and how to solve them. But the water chemistry of an aquarium is a complicated subject, and I would recommend everybody who wants to know more about this topic, or has special requirements, to read specialist literature on this subject.

When you set up your aquarium, the following tests are necessary: pH, KH, NO_2 (nitrite).

Plants

The plants in the aquarium should not only be beautiful to look at but also serve a biological purpose by producing oxygen. They absorb nutrients (e.g. waste products from the fish) from the water and thus

Jouni Jaakkola

Given the correct conditions plants can grow tremendously, like this *Microsorium pteropus* "Windelöw" which has been taken out of the aquarium to show its size.

help in keeping the aquarium clean. The plants also have other positive effects, such as providing small fishes with hiding places and offering spawning sites for a lot of species.

Whether you want to have plants in your aquarium will depend on what kind of fishes you choose and/or what kind of biotope you want to imitate. Some species (such as many different kinds of cichlids and goldfish) eat plants or dig a lot, and are therefore unsuitable for planted aquaria. If you want to imitate nature in your aquarium then plants are often a far from obvious choice. In the Great Lakes of Malawi and Tanganyika, and in some biotopes in South America (e.g. where you find discus), there are hardly any plants at all (except for the ones that are attached to roots and hang down from the shore into the water). In aquaria containing species from such habitats you can create a beautiful decor consisting of rocks, wood, and a decorative background. A more efficient filter can substitute the biological function of the plants.

There are, however, few aquaria that can compete in beauty with a

Ole Pedersen

Nymphea lotus (green form).

21

well-kept planted aquarium, even though this means some hard work. Below I have listed a few points that need to be considered when setting up a planted aquarium.

1. Light — plants need plenty of light (see EQUIPMENT — lighting) even though this may vary between different plant species (see information about different plants).

2. Water — most plants get on well in a water that is neither too hard nor too soft (KH 5-12°) and neutral (pH 6.5-7.2).

3. Bottom heating — plants may suffer from "cold feet" (see EQUIPMENT — heating).

4. The bottom substrate — a 6-10 cm layer of gravel that does not contain calcium and has a grain size of 2 mm is ideal.

5. Nutrients (point 1) — initially there may not be enough nutrients in the water to sustain the plants. There are, however, excellent products on the market that you mix into the gravel or use as fertilizer on different areas of the gravel.

6. Transportation pots — some aquarium plants are cultivated in small plastic pots that are filled up with mineral wool. This reduces the risk of damage during transportation. Do not forget, however, to remove the pot and the mineral wool before planting.

7. How many? — plant plenty of plants in an aquarium that has just been set up.

8. Planting — cut off damaged leaves and parts from the stalk. Spread out the roots, and if they are too long (more than 3 cm) — cut them off. Plant carefully so that roots do not get damaged.

9. Nutrients (point 2) — the water may lack some plant nutrients such as iron and different kinds of trace elements. Use a complete fertilizer (better than the products that contain only iron) for aquarium plants, available at aquarium stores. But use fertilizer with moderation, otherwise only the algae will prosper.

10. Houseplants — a number of non-aquatic houseplants (e.g. *Spathiphyllum wallisii*) are sold in

Ole Pedersen

Spathiphyllum wallisii is not an aquarium plant and is better kept in a paludarium.

the aquarium trade. These cannot survive in the aquarium and must be avoided.

11. Regular water changes — plants, like fishes, enjoy regular water changes.

12. CO_2 — a good CO_2 (carbon dioxide) system will increase plant growth and make them reproduce more rapidly, as CO_2 is a necessary building-block in the metabolic processes of the plants. In addition CO_2 stabilizes the pH value at a level that is good for the plants. Always bear in mind, however, that if the buffering capacity of the water is low (viz. a KH of 3° or lower) the pH will sink rapidly if CO_2 is added to the water. This could be hazardous to the fish, so you should always increase the KH, for instance with calcium (see WATER) to a level of 4-5° when using CO_2.

Nowadays there is an excellent selection of different species of aquarium plants on the market, offering something for every taste.

The same rule can be applied here as when buying fish (see BUYING FISH): buy only a few kinds of plants and a correspondingly larger number of every species instead. Plant each species in a separate group. You can also buy plants that are attached to a piece of wood or rock; these are very decorative and handy. You can, however, easily make one yourself by attaching a suitable plant (e.g. *Anubias*, *Microsorum*, and/or *Vesicularia*) to a piece of wood or rock with the help of a rubber band or piece of nylon thread. In a short time the roots of the plant will have attached them-

It is possible to buy plants that are attached to a piece of wood or, like the *Microsorium pteropus* on the photo, on a rock.

selves to the wood or rock.

There are plenty of examples of good, beautiful, and comparatively hardy plants, some of which are depicted in the photos at the end of this book.

Algae

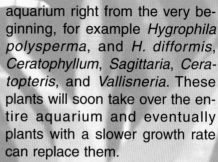

Algae present a serious problem to many hobbyists. Every aquarium is unique. You cannot set up two aquaria under identical conditions. In the one aquarium you might notice a significant growth of algae, in the other there might be no algae at all. There are, however, some rules that can be applied.

As I have mentioned earlier, the aquarium should be sited where it will not be exposed to direct sunlight. It is also a good idea to buy some algae-eating fish right from the start, for example some *Otocinclus* species, *Crossochelius siamensis*, together with some *Ancistrus* species. The last of these may, however, cause some damage to the plants if there is insufficient algae to feed them. Other species, suitable for larger aquaria, are *Hypostomus plecostomus* and, for very large aquaria, *Glyptoperichtys gibbiceps* (sailfin plec). A common feature of all algae-eating species is that they usually eat only green algae.

A very good trick for avoiding algae is to plant fast-growing plants in the aquarium right from the very beginning, for example *Hygrophila polysperma*, and *H. difformis*, *Ceratophyllum*, *Sagittaria*, *Ceratopteris*, and *Vallisneria*. These plants will soon take over the entire aquarium and eventually plants with a slower growth rate can replace them.

If your intention is not to have plants in the aquarium, you can reduce the amount of algae by keeping the light turned off for a while. This would not work in an aquarium with plants, since they would die.

The most common reason for problems with algae is excess nutrients caused by overfeeding the fishes, and/or by having too many fishes in the aquarium and/or by not performing water changes on a regular basis. Hence it is preferable to have a small number of fish at the beginning (preferably algae-eaters) and not to feed them too frequently.

There are also algicides on the market. These, however, should be regarded as a last resort. It is true that they reduce the algae, but they do not, however, get rid of the causes of algae growth, and the algae will soon be back again. Furthermore algicides sometimes reduce not only the growth of the algae but also that of the plants as well.

The sailfin plec is a good algae eating fish for very big aquaria.

Kjell Fohrman

Equipment

You will need various equipment — such as a filter, immersion heater, lighting etc. — to keep the aquarium running and provide a suitable environment for the fishes. Most of the equipment that you will need is electrical, and the combination of electricity and water can be highly dangerous. Hence you

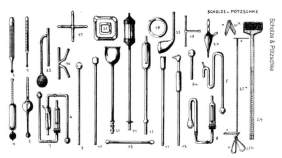

70 years ago aquarium keeping equipment was somewhat different than it is now, or...?

should check that the products are approved as suitable from a safety point of view. For safety reasons you may want to use a circuit breaker that switches of the power if something goes wrong.

One problem with equipment is that it is unattractive if visible in the aquarium. A filter attached to the end glass is not particularly beautiful, and as far as I am concerned, it is not much better than a plastic diver! If you have a background in your aquarium then you may be able to conceal the equipment behind that, otherwise you should try to position equipment such that it is concealed behind rocks, a big piece of wood, or a group of plants.

Filter

Whether you should have a filter for the aquarium, and, if so, how big it should be, depends very much on the number of fishes and their sizes and whether or not you want to grow plants.

An aquarium can function perfectly well without any kind of filtration. I have a good friend who once had a 250-litre tank without any filtration. He fed the fish spar-

To be able to keep *Catoprion mento* in an aquarium, you need a very large tank (min. 250 cm) with a very effective filter.

Rhadinocentrus ornatus is a peaceful, lively schooling fish, but has proven to be sensitive.

ingly (they lived mainly on algae) and merely replaced the water that evaporated. In this aquarium there were just two fishes (a pair of *Chalinochromis brichardi*) that were 8 cm long. When they bred, the juveniles were removed from the aquarium.

In most cases, however, you want to have more fishes than that in the aquarium, and consequently you will need a filter. The reason is partly that the water needs to be mechanically filtered (to remove particles that cloud the water) and partly that you must maintain a biological balance in the water (for this you need a large area of filter material where nitrogen cycle bacteria can grow). These bacteria will break down the organic pollutants in the water.

The filter can also be used to ensure an adequate oxygen supply. The latter is very important for species, which in nature typically live in fast-flowing or turbulent water (e.g. many cichlid and catfish species) and are thus adapted to a life in water high in oxygen. You can produce water that is high in oxygen by placing the outlet close to the water's surface. A common misconception is that the bubbles from the airstone produce a lot of oxygen. This is wrong. The bubbles stirs up the surface of the water and this facilitates the absorption of oxygen from the air into the water, but it is far more efficient to place the outlet of the pump close to the water's surface than to use airstones.

An aquarium pump from 1930 in the Scholze & Pötzschke mailorder catalogue.

There are two main types of filter: internal filters and external filters.

The advantages of an internal filter are that it is comparatively cheap, simple to install in the tank, and easy to clean. The disadvantages are that it takes up a lot of space in the aquarium and must be cleaned more frequently than an outside filter.

The advantages of an external filter are that it takes up very little place in the aquarium and does not have to be cleaned very often (at the most once every six months, given the right filter material). If you want to influence the chemical composition of the water it is easy to put suitable filter material into the filter canister. The disadvantages are that these filters are a little bit more expensive, are more complicated to clean, and need space outside the aquarium. For an aquarium of 300 litres you need a filter canister of at least 4 litres capacity.

How efficient a filter is depends mainly on what type of filter material you use. The sponge that is used in internal filters is often too small. It is better if you make one yourself as shown in the diagram. The filter material should never be washed in hot water since this will kill the bacteria that help to keep the water clean.

You can use different kinds of filter material in external filters for maximum effectiveness. So-called bio-balls are highly effective; another good filter material is zeolite. You can also put material that influences the water chemistry in external filters, for instance peat, to make the water acid. You can also put activated carbon in the canister to chemically filter out some medicines (after medication). When cleaning the outside filter, only part of the material should be replaced or even cleaned, or else you will kill all the useful bacteria in the filter.

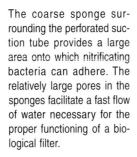

The coarse sponge surrounding the perforated suction tube provides a large area onto which nitrificating bacteria can adhere. The relatively large pores in the sponges facilitate a fast flow of water necessary for the proper functioning of a biological filter.

A filter that has been shut off for some time (a couple of hours), for instance during a power cut, must never be restarted without the filter being cleaned (this is true of outside filters in particular since

Distichodus fasciolatus is an extremely large fish that mainly feeds on vegetable content (fibres) and pollutes the water a lot, therefore it is necessary to have a very effective filter.

they have a big canister). Otherwise the filter may release dangerous substances into the water, and the entire aquarium can be affected.

I have deliberately not mentioned the undergravel filter (which makes the water circulate through the gravel which acts as a biological filter material) since it is not used extensively anymore. Today there are far more efficient filter materials than gravel, and an undergravel filter might, at the most, be regarded as a complement to other filtration methods.

Regardless what kind of filter you use, you must never forget that no filter can replace regular water changes (see MAINTENANCE).

The red variant of *Colisa labiosa* is rather new in the trade.

Mark Smith

Heating

Most aquarium fishes originate from tropical climates and enjoy temperatures ranging from 24-26° C. The filter and lighting contribute to raising the temperature, but in most cases this will not be enough and you will need an immersion heater.

The most common type of immersion heater is a glass tube with a thermostatic built-in heater element. These, however, have a disadvantage: since hot water rises there can be quite a difference in temperature between the water layers. A powerful filter that circulates the water can partially compensate for this.

In planted aquaria the plants will sometimes suffer from "cold feet". To avoid this you may wish to use a heating cable that is placed under the gravel. Since hot water rises, this causes circulation, which sucks nutrient-laden water down into the gravel for the plants. A great disadvantage with this kind of heating is that it is much more expensive than an ordinary immersion heater. Nowadays there are also cheaper kinds of substrate heating on the market — ask at your local aquarium store. One way of avoiding "cold feet" is to place an isolating sheet of styrofoam on the bottom of the aquarium or between the aquarium and the bench.

As an approximate measure, the wattage of the heating should be 1/3 to 1/2 watts/litre of aquarium water given a room temperature off 20-22° C.

Tank covers

Some aquarium hobbyists use cover glasses on their aquaria, others do not. It is important to remember that the glass reduces the lighting to some extent and also blocks some of the light wavelengths that are important for the plants.

If you decide not to use a cover glass, some of the water in the aquarium will evaporate (the greater the surface area and the more powerful the water circulation, the greater the evaporation), and increase the humidity of the air in the room where the aquarium stands. This is, however, often an advantage, since today it is common for the air in centrally-heated houses to be too dry. As well as the evaporation of the water, heat will also disappear from the aquarium, which increases the expense of heating the aquarium. An aquarium hood will reduce evaporation and heat loss, but if you use cover glasses you will keep down the evaporation to a minimum.

A disadvantage of not using any tank cover is that some species may jump out of the aquarium — killies and rainbow fishes are, for instance, good jumpers.

Lighting

The kind of lighting you want to use often depends on whether or not you want to keep plants in the aquarium. Plants require a lot of light (though this may vary from species to species), but fishes do not have particularly high requirements for lighting and some prefer dimly-lit conditions. In plant aquariums aquaria mercury-vapour (HQL) or metal halogen lighting (HQI) will be the most suitable; these kinds of lighting are, unfortunately, very expensive (especially the HQI). Nowadays there are so called low-energy bulbs that may be sufficient for very small aquaria. In a planted aquarium, however, bulbs are not enough.

The most common form of lighting is fluorescent tubes, and these are often sufficient — provided that they are designed for promoting aquarium plant growth, that there are enough of them, that the reflectors are effective (these can be bought separately), and that the aquarium does not contain plant species that have a very high light requirement (see the plant chapter at the end of this book). One type of fluorescent tube that brings out good colour in the fish but is relatively soft, and therefore not much good for plants, is the so-called Grolux tube.

When using fluorescent tubes you should keep in mind the fact that their effect gradually decreases, and for this reason they should be replaced once a year, even if they are still working. You will achieve the most attractive effect if you place the tubes at the front and the middle of the aqua-

Ole Pedersen

29

Barbus rhomboocellatus is a peaceful schooling fish that prefers aquaria with subdued light.

All Synodontis (photo. S. longirostris) have long barbels and easily get stuck if caught with a wide-meshed net. It is better to use a fine-meshed net when catching catfishes.

rium, not at the back. Unfortunately most covers on the market today are not constructed so that the tubes will be at the front of the aquarium. For an aquarium that is 40-50 cm deep and 40 cm wide it will be sufficient to have two fluorescent tubes that are almost as long as the aquarium. If the aquarium is 10 cm deeper or higher then you need one additional tube.

The aquarium lighting should be switched on for a continuous period of 10-12 hours a day. It makes sense to use a timer. You cannot compensate for less powerful lighting by having the light on for a longer time. The plants (and fishes) need time to rest. Having the light on too long usually leads to uncontrolled algae growth.

Other equipment

Other equipment that is needed includes a magnetic algae remover or scraper, a thermometer (not a mercury one for environmental reasons), different kinds of test kits and water conditioners/treatments (see WATER). You will also need some nets (one for each aquarium) with different size of mesh (e.g. fine-meshed for catfish, wide-meshed for other fishes), a siphon hose (about 1.5 metres long with an inside diameter of about 12 mm, and also a bucket. For larger aquaria you will need a hose that reaches from the aquarium to the drain and the faucet. It is also a good idea to buy a gravel-cleaner from your local dealer, but you can also easily make one yourself: take an empty, well-cleaned, plastic fizzy drink bottle (1.5-2 litres), cut off the bottom and attach the hose to the top. Start it by using the siphon principle and apply it to the bottom of the aquarium. The waste products will leave the bottom, while the gravel will stay.

It is also a good idea to have a small quarantine aquarium by the side of the main aquarium, this can also be used to treat sick fish and to let bullied ones recover.

Food

In nature all fishes are adapted to feed on certain kinds of food. Some species are more versatile then others, which are more specialized. For practical reasons we deal with the following main groups in this book.

Carnivores — species that live on other vertebrates or invertebrates.

Omnivores — species that eat all kinds of food.

Herbivores — species that eat plants.

The fish species in the different groups often have different body shapes and different teeth that have been developed to "catch" the food they prefer to eat. Even more important, the digestive system, in particular the intestine, may be adapted to a certain kind of food. Piscivorous fishes (in the carnivore group) that live on other fishes often have a very short intestine and a large stomach with room for large prey. This kind of food is easy to digest, and so they do not need a long intestine; the intestine of omnivores is longer. The intestine of herbivores is extremely long, an adaptation to permit the breakdown of fibrous material that is hard to digest.

Fishes are cold-blooded animals, which cannot make use of fats from warm-blooded animals (e.g. mammals) in the same way as they can with those from other aquatic creatures, hence animal fats can be harmful.

Today there is a large variety of high quality foods containing most of the vitamins that the fishes need. There are even food types that are adapted to certain needs, for instance those containing green food for herbivores, and special food tablets for catfish.

The problem is usually not finding a suitable type of food, but a

Pseudacanthicus leopardus (L 114) is an omnivore feeding on any aquarium fare offered.

Cyphotilapia frontosa, a piscivore, feeds mainly on fishes in the wild, in the aquarium they also eat other foods.

31

tendency to feed too much! In nature the fish have to work hard to find food; in the aquarium everything is "handed to them on a plate". This is an existence to which they adapt very fast, and they often grow much bigger in the aquarium than they would in nature. In addition the quality of the water will deteriorate faster (and there is a risk of pH drops and problems with algae) if you feed too much. So never overfeed. It is sufficient to feed twice a day (more often for fry), and never more than what the fishes will eat within two minutes.

Many fishes are mainly nocturnal, like *Acanthopsis dialuzona*, and must be fed in the evening.

Nowadays there is available a large variety of high quality foods containing most of the vitamins.

Even if you find one food type that contains all the necessary vitamins, proteins, fats, fibre, etc. in the proportions that are exactly right for your fish, I think it is better to vary the food. Fish that get used to eating different kinds of food are, in my experience, hardier and are not affected so often by diseases as fish that get the same kind of food all the time.

I would also recommend that you always drop most of the food at a particular spot, but that you also feed a little in another spot. This is because some fishes may dominate the whole aquarium, while others are a little more reserved and may thus not be allowed to come forward to eat at the main spot.

You must also consider the fact that different species live at different levels in the aquarium, and if you feed only floating foods the fishes living at the bottom may not get an opportunity to eat.

Whatever kind of food you will choose, it is important that you store it properly and that you do not keep it too long once opened since the beneficial vitamins will deteriorate very fast. If for instance, you place an open food container above the lighting fittings, it will be only a matter of

Mark Smith

Kjell Fohrman

hours before the food will be useless as regards vitamins. Instead you should place it somewhere dry and cool (always with the lid on) and it will stay useable much longer. It makes sense to have a small can with food beside the aquarium and to refill this when empty.

The following are the main types of food on the market:

Flake food. By far the most common type of food. Nowadays most brands are of very high quality. There are also different types of flake food that are designed for different fish species. There are even special foods that will enhance the natural colours of the fishes.

Granular food. A very good food that is suitable for fish that are not too big. Sometimes there is also a practical dosage button on the lid, which makes it possible for you to avoid touching the food with your hands and also prevents overfeeding.

Pellets. The most common food type for medium-sized and large fishes, together with pond fishes. There are even special foods that will enhance the natural colours of the fishes.

Frozen food. There are a lot of different varieties of frozen foods. They are a good complement to flake foods. I especially like *Cyclops*, which is a excellent food for small fish and fry. The most common frozen food on the market is bloodworm, which is a good sup-

plementary food for most fishes. A warning, however, must be issued: Do not feed bloodworms to algae-eating fish that live in waters with a high pH (e.g. Malawi and Tanganyika cichlids). There is an high risk of causing diseases, just in these fishes.

Scatophagus argus is a unselective omnivore that eats flake food, pellets, frozen and live foods, and plants.

Trichogaster trichopterus (albino-form of the blue Gourami shown) accepts most aquarium foods without any problem.

You must also bear in mind that bloodworm can cause an allergic reaction in human beings. Given these problems I use bloodworms only to a very small extent. I prefer to feed with *Cyclops*, brine shrimp, *Gammarus*, mysis, and other shrimps.

Frozen food is relatively low in vitamins, since the frozen organisms themselves often are vitamin poor. Today there are, however, special liquid vitamin supplements designed to be added to frozen food before feeding.

Freeze-dried food. Freeze-dried foods are composed of organisms that have been freeze-dried. I myself hardly never ever use this kind of food, instead I prefer frozen food. Freeze-dried bloodworms can cause contact allergic reactions to a greater extent than frozen ones.

Food tablets. Good foods that are especially suitable for catfishes and fishes active at night. Place a few tablets on a spot (always the same one) in the aquarium after the lighting has been switched off at night. There are tablets that are adhesive and can be attached to the glass (e.g. for *Otocinclus* species), and those designed to be placed on the bottom (e.g. for *Corydoras* species). There are vegetable-food tablets (for algae-eating species, e.g. for *Ancistrus*) and omnivore-food tablets (e.g. for *Corydoras*).

Live food. In the old days, no self-respecting aquarium hobbyist would be satisfied with himself if he or she was not out in the nature at least a couple of days a week to catch his or her own living food. Today there is high quality dry and frozen foods on the market, and it is not more absolute necessary, even if the fish, of course, appreciate it. Foods that you can catch yourself are, for instance, *Cyclops*, *Daphnia*, and glassworms. When breeding fish it is very usual that you hatch your own brine shrimp to feed the fry with. Eggs of brine shrimp for hatching can be bought in the aquarium store. The quality and the price might vary considerably, and the best thing to do is to get in contact with an experienced hobbyist (in an aquarium club) that you can ask for advice.

All killifishes (photo *Aphyosemion bivittatum*) need to be fed with live food.

Maintenance

Owning an aquarium also means a responsibility to your pets — the fishes.

The aquarium fish is an easily-maintained pet that does not require a lot of attention. Regular maintenance and care of the aquarium, however, is an absolute necessity to keep the fishes healthy in the long term and make the aquarium an attractive sight.

It is of the utmost importance for the well-being of the aquarium that you perform regular partial water changes; no filter can replace this. It is also very important not to feed too much. 95% of all problems with aquaria are caused by these two factors.

Sometimes you hear of hobbyists who have kept their fish in peak condition for quite some time without even changing water (apart from adding water to compensate for evaporation). I once found a small breeding aquarium, which had been stored away for quite some time. I had not removed the gravel, and hence there was still some water in it. In one of the corners the gravel level was a little lower, creating an area of about 10 x 3 x 2 cm containing water, where a very lively young fish of about 3 cm was still living. It was jumping about when caught

from the stinking water. It was immediately transferred to a normal aquarium with perfect water conditions where it died instantly! We all learn by our mistakes.

The reason it died was that fishes often are very adaptable and can get used to very poor water conditions (if these arise slowly). The problem is that it is often difficult to introduce other fishes (that are used to other water conditions). When you eventually performs a partial water change, the fish will not stand the shock. The pH in the aquarium

Ctenops nobilis, like any other fish, needs regular water changes.

might be around 6, while that of the tap water is around 8 (the Malawi juvenile mentioned above died of the shock). It is also not possible to put medicine in such an aquarium.

Daily routines. Feed with moderation once or twice a day (see under FOOD, above). When feeding, make it your practice to ob-

35

serve the behaviour of the fishes for several minutes. Are they breathing normally (see DIS-EASES, below)? Are they as hungry as usual, are all of them eating, etc.? If one fish refuses to eat, it may be the first sign that something is wrong. Check temperatures, and that all equipment is working?

Weekly routines. Once a week you should clean the glasses with an algae scraper, remove dead parts of plants and generally attend to the plants a little, and siphon off mulm from the bottom. If necessary clean the filter as well (change the filter material if it has deteriorated in function) and, above all, perform a partial water change with suitably prepared (matured/treated/conditioned, as required) tap water. It is appropriate to change 10-35% of the water every week. How much you should change depends on how many fishes you have in the aquarium and how big they are, how large the aquarium is, and also if the fishes have a high oxygen requirement. In a planted aquarium with only few fishes you will not need to change that much water (10-20%). In aquaria with big fishes, however, a lot more (30-35%) is required. Always make sure you switch off electrical equipment such as immersion heaters and filters before cleaning.

Test also the water frequently (see WATER-Tests).

Bi-monthly routines (or more frequently if necessary). The cover glasses, if you have them, and the light fittings should be cleaned. Limescale may be removed by using vinegar, or a lime deposit remover, e.g. as sold for coffee machines. Rinse the cover glasses carefully before you put them back on the aquarium.

Take care that none of the liquid drops into the water.

Vacation routines. Unlike many other pets, fishes usually do not constitute a problem if you are going on vacation. They can manage very well without food for about two weeks. If you are staying away for a longer period, you can always use an automatic feeding machine (experiment to get the right "dosage" before you leave) or let your neighbour, who is already watering your plants, give your fish a little food. I must stress the word "a little", because it is extremely common for your neighbour to feel sorry for the fishes and, with the best of intentions, give them too much food, with a disaster as a consequence. Hence, provide measured portions or give very detailed instructions.

Before you go on vacation you should also perform a partial water change. Also consider the fact that a closed room may get very hot in the summer. This will affect the aquarium water too, which is bad for the fishes, so always close the curtains and/or blinds to reduce the risk, and ask your neighbour to air the room.

Breeding

During the course of evolution fishes have developed different ways of breeding, depending on the environment they live in and the way this itself came into being. A number of main groups may be distinguished.

Bubble-nest builders: These fishes build a nest at the surface with the help of "saliva" and bits of plants. During the spawning the male entwines his body around the female and spits the eggs up into the nest. After that the male watches over the spawn, which hatches within 24-30 hours after

of days. An example of an egg-scattering species is the zebra danio (*Brachydanio rerio*).

Astyanax mexicanus is one of many egg-scatterers.

A male *Colisa chuna* guarding his bubble-nest.

the spawning. Good examples of the bubble-nest builders are the gourami species.

Egg-scatterers: Fishes that spawn in the open water. The eggs fall down among rocks (or into the gravel) or stick to plants. The spawn will hatch within a couple

Substratum spawners: Fish species that attach their eggs to different kinds of objects (= substrates), e.g. the panes of the aquarium, on rocks, in a cave etc. The spawn will often hatch within a couple of days. A lot of cichlid species belong to this group. Some substrate spawners abandon their eggs to their fate after spawning, but others (**Substratum brooders**), notably cichlids, guard both eggs and fry.

Mouthbrooders: After/during spawning the female gathers the eggs into her mouth and broods them for 2-5 weeks. During this period the eggs develop into fry. When the fry are fully-developed she releases them. Some species will even take them in again at any sign of danger. This is the most

The orange chromide (*Etroplus maculatus*) is a substrate brooder which deposits the eggs on a stone or a root.

The killie *Notobranchius foerschi* is an annual fish, which means that they have a short life.

common form of mouthbrooding, but sometimes the male or both parents brood, and sometimes the eggs are attached to a substrate and only the larvae/fry are brooded. The mouthbrooders include a lot of cichlid species but also some catfishes and a few labyrinth fishes.

Livebearers: The species in this group produce fully-formed living fry. A lot of the most common aquarium fishes are represented in this group, e.g. swordtails and platys.

Many of the common aquarium fishes, like this sailfin molly (*Poecilia velifera*), are livebearers.

Annual fishes: In nature these species often live in pools of water that dry up completely once a year. As a result the fishes die, but before this happens they bury their eggs in the bottom substrate, to hatch during the next rainy period. Some of the killifishes belong to this group.

It is not at all unusual to see the fishes in your aquarium spawn, and, of course, it is a real experience to see a pair of cichlids watch over their "kids" in the aquarium, or to have your first guppy or swordtail fry. This is without doubt one of the major highlights of the hobby. What to do to get the fishes to breed varies from species to species, of course: some are easy, others almost impossible, and it is totally impossible to describe them all in a small book like this. I would advise you to read the specialist literature about the fishes you own, read about other breeders' experiences in the various aquarium magazines, and join an aquarium club to get advice.

Diseases

It does not matter how well you take care of your fishes, you cannot totally prevent them from falling victim to diseases, even though it is quite unusual for them to fall sick. I have had about 10 aquaria running in recent years, and on only one occasion have the fishes fallen ill. The reason for this was that the immersion heater was broken and as a consequence the temperature had fallen below 20° C before I noticed the problem.

You will most probably discover if a fish is sick when you feed them. A healthy fish is always hungry, and therefore it is important to take a minute a day to observe your fish while feeding.

The most common reason for a fish becoming ill is that it is exposed to some kind of stress. There are many reasons for a fish becoming stressed: bad water quality, sudden changes in the water chemistry/quality or incorrect water chemistry, incorrect temperature, bad maintenance, incorrect feeding, attacks by other fishes, other diseases, too few hiding-places, incorrect lighting, transportation, etc. Appropriate treatment can often cure a sick fish, but you also need to find out why it fell sick (the cause of the stress). When (if) you find out the cause (it is not always that easy) you must, of course, correct whatever is wrong, otherwise there is a great risk that the fish will fall sick again very soon.

You also need to draw a distinction between toxicity (poisoning) and infectious diseases (which, however, may well spread more rapidly if the fishes are already affected by toxicity). Poisoning is not a disease in itself, but fishes may become diseased as a result of such external influences. A typical feature of toxicity is that it suddenly affects every fish (or most of the fishes) in the aquarium, while infectious diseases initially affect only a few fishes, and then gradually spread to the others. Other signs of poisoning are hyperventilation (very common); the gills, and sometimes the whole body, become dark; jerky swimming etc. There are several possible reasons for the poisoning: the most common reasons are too much nitrite and/or an incorrect pH value (see WATER for more information). Poisoning can, however, also be caused by tobacco smoke, insect spray, paint being applied (fumes) in the room where the aquarium stands, or even by the use of the wrong kind of wood in the aquarium. In the latter case, changing 50% of the water, removing the root, and heavy aeration can solve the problem.

It is, as already mentioned, pretty easy to diagnose that the fishes are suffering from poisoning since the problem often affects all the fishes (or at least the majority); the problem also manifests rapidly and the fishes hyperventilate. It is often harder to diagnose an infectious disease in the aquarium, since this will usually appear slowly and affect only a few fish in the beginning. And the use of medication is usually most effective if applied right at the beginning of the outbreak.

When medicating fishes you should always remember to:

1. Perform a partial water change before medicine is added to the water.

2. Clean the filter before medicating.

3. Increase the oxygen supply by directing the filter outlet towards the surface of the water and/or providing additional sources of aeration, as some medicines reduce the content of oxygen in the water (they may also kill the beneficial bacteria).

4. Follow the instructions on the medicine packaging.

5. Always look at the "best before date". Medicines may lose their effectiveness with age. Once opened the container should be closed again tightly and kept in a cool place.

6. Never medicate unnecessarily. Medication is a chemical stress factor that also might disturb the biological balance of the aquarium. Therefore always supervise the aquarium the first hours after you have added the medicine.

7. Avoid medicating as a preventive measure — apart from in exceptional cases.

8. Check the water parameters before adding medicine to the aquarium.

9. Never filter with active carbon during medication.

10. Bear in mind that most diseases are stress-related to some degree, and eliminate whatever is causing the stress.

11. If possible, medicate fishes in a special "hospital tank", as some medications will kill beneficial bacteria in the normal aquarium and lead to nitrite problems.

12. Sometimes salt is recommended as a medication. But note that salt should be used only with salt-tolerant species.

Below is a short list of some of the commonest diseases that may appear in your aquarium:

White spot disease (*Ichthyophthirius multifilis*)

Symptoms: small (0.03-1.5 mm) white spots spread all over the body (mainly on and around the fins). White spot disease is caused by a unicellular parasite and is fairly common, very contagious,

Mary Bailey

If a fish has "white spot disease" you usually find white spots spread all over the body, but mainly on and around the fins.

and fatal if not treated in time.

Treatment: Easy to cure. There are several very effective medicines available from the aquarium store. When adding medicine, the water temperature should not be below 26° C for tropical species.

Velvet (*Oodinium*)

Symptoms: Caused by a unicellular flagellate. The fishes have grey or yellowish velvet-like (or dusty) coating of very small, very close-packed, spots.

Treatment: Very effective medicines are available from the aquarium store. The water temperature should not be below 26° C when the medicine is added. It is also a good idea to add 5 ml of marine or rock salt per 100 litres of water. Excluding all light for a few days can also cure Oodinium.

Skin Slime Disease (*Costia, Trichodina, Chilodonella*)

Symptoms: These protozoan parasites cause a thin milky grey film on the body of the fish. Severe attacks cause bloodshot red spots on the body. Often the fishes will scratch on the rocks and gravel and keep their fins folded.

Treatment: Available from the aquarium store. Can be treated with some of the medications for white spot disease but a longer treatment is necessary. The water temperature should not be below 26° C during the treatment. It also makes sense to add 5 ml marine or rock salt per 100 litres of water.

Fungus (e.g. *Saprolegnia*)

Symptoms: Often affects fishes that are already physically injured or in bad shape. Affected fishes develop a "woolly" or "fluffy" whitish coating (that gets darker and darker), all over or in patches on the body. It is not particularly contagious. The affected fish can be removed from the aquarium and placed in a hospital aquarium, where treatment takes place.

Treatment: There are very effec-

Fungus is easy to diagnose but sometimes difficult to treat.

tive medicines available from the aquarium store. Raise the temperature a little and add marine or rock salt.

Mouth "fungus" (a bacterial infection caused by *Flexibacter columnaris*)

Symptoms: Grey-white "fluffy" spots on the head (especially around the mouth), on the body, and on the fins. These spots eventually transform into lesions. This disease is very contagious and can wipe out the whole fish population within a few days.

Treatment: Use a medicine that contains Nifurpirinol (Nitrofuradantin, Furazolidone) (only from

41

the vet in some countries), increase the water circulation in the aquarium. Add marine or rock salt. Isolate infected fishes in a quarantine aquarium and treat them. Never keep infected fish together with healthy ones.

Bacterial fin rot

Symptoms: Bacterial disease that is triggered by bad environmental conditions in the aquarium. At first the edges of the fins turn pale, and this pale colour may spread with the fin becoming eroded.

Treatment: Use a medicine that contains Nifurpirinol (Nitrofura-dantin, Furazolidone) (only from the vet in some countries). Add marine or rock salt. Improve water quality.

Neon tetra disease (*Pleisto-phora*)

Symptoms: In particular affects neons and cardinals and other tetras and is dangerous and contagious. The colour of the affected fish will turn pale.

Treatment: Hard to cure, medication with Nifurpirinol (see bacterial fin rot) has in some cases proven to be effective.

Particularly sensitive species

Some species are more sensitive than others. Even though it is impossible to mention them all, I would like to include a number of very common species that are considered to be "problematic" (if they are not given the right environment).

Colisa species (e.g. the dwarf gourami) need a calm environment in the aquarium, with dark hiding-places. The filtration must not be too powerful. They also like a slightly higher temperature and appreciate frozen food such as *Cyclops*.

The cardinal tetra (*Paracheir-*

The cardinal tetra (*Paracheirodon axelrodi*) is more delicate than the Neon tetra and must be acclimatized to the aquarium very slowly.

odon axelrodi) is considerably more delicate than, for example, the neon tetra, and very easily gets neon tetra sickness. They cannot stand any major changes as far as water conditions are concerned. New fishes must be acclimatized (see BUYING FISHES) very slowly.

The clown loach (*Botia macracanthus*), the Ram or South American butterfly cichlid (*Mikrogeophagus ramirezi*), and hatchet-fishes (e.g. *Carnegiella*) are all examples of fish that are very susceptible to white spot disease, especially following transportation, hence special care is required when acclimatizing these fishes.

The guppy (*Poecilia reticulata*) is bred in incredibly large numbers in Asia, and has been inbred to such an extent that this once hardy beginner's fish is nowadays sometimes a delicate one. Try to find guppies that have been bred within your own country.

The black molly (*Poecilia sphenops*) and sailfin molly (*Poecilia velifera*) are also bred very intensively in Asia. They are bred in rather warm water that is very salty, and hence you may sometimes have to add some salt to your aquarium. Furthermore the temperature must be around 27-28° C. These conditions are hard on the plants.

Some popular aquarium fishes, such as *Poecilia sphenops*, are bred in rather warm and salty water, which makes it difficult to adapt them to normal aquarium water.

Cichlids from lakes Malawi and Tanganyika, and a lot of catfish as well, do not appreciate heavy metals in the water. They seem to be especially sensitive to copper. Thus, always bear in mind that some medicines may contain copper (look at the table of contents). Domestic pipework is often made

Many catfishes (photo *Hypoptopoma* species) are sensitive to heavy metals (such as copper) in the water.

from copper, and it is wise to run the tap for a while before using it for fishes, so that you use water that has not "stood" in contact with copper. If the boiler and/or the pipework in the house are new or if your water is very soft. I recommend that you are very cautious about using water from the hot water system when you change water.

Some fishes e.g. *Corydoras* are sensitive to salt in the water. Therefore always check if the fishes you have in your aquarium are sensitive to salt before you salt for any reason.

Some medical treatments call for salt in the water, but please note that some fishes, such as all *Corydoras* species (photo: *Corydoras ellisae*), are sensitive to salt.

Buying fishes

What would an aquarium be like if there were no fishes in it?! Fortunately there are a lot to choose from. The later pages of this book introduce more than 500 different species and that is only a fraction of what there is on the market. There are a lot of different combinations possible, some species should be kept in pairs, some in shoals etc. Below I have listed some issues you must consider before making up your mind what to keep:

* Do you want a biotope aquarium (with fishes and plants from a single special habitat) or a community tank with fishes and plants that get on well together but may come from lots of different places and habitats.

* Big fish will eat small fish (this is often a problem!).

* The fish that are sold in the aquarium store are often juveniles; find out how big they will get.

* How large is your aquarium? Big fishes need a lot of space. Aggressive fishes must have a big aquarium sometimes to themselves.

* Do you want to have plants in your aquarium or not? If you do, avoid fishes that eat plants.

* Some species require acid water, others prefer alkaline water. What is the water like where you live, will it suit the fishes you are considering?

Without doubt there are further questions that need to be asked; the most important thing, however, is that you consider what your aquarium should be like before you set it up. Visit different aquarium stores and ask questions; if possible, visit an aquarium exhibition and/or public aquarium.

When you have thought everything through, then, and only then, is it time to buy the fishes; but here again there are points that need to be taken into consideration.

* Visit an aquarium store with a large assortment. If the aquaria are nice and clean (no or only a

small amount of algae on the glasses) the chances are greater that the quality of the fish will be better than in a store where the aquaria are not even being cleaned.

* Never buy sick fishes or even healthy fishes that are mixed with sick fishes in the store. If they are hanging in a corner or are breathing heavily, something is wrong. Another bad sign is if the fins are not extended.

* Do not buy too few specimens of every species, and this is true not only for fishes that live in shoals. An aquarium with few species but multiple specimens of every species is always more beautiful than the other way around. Furthermore, even some (but not all) territorial fishes (e.g. mouthbrooding cichlids) will be less aggressive if there are multiple specimens of every species.

* Do not forget to take the maximum size of the fish into consideration, its requirements as regards pH etc. If no details are provided on the tank, do not hesitate to ask.

* Right from the start you should buy some algae-eating fish (see ALGAE).

* Start with a small number of fishes (see WATER).

How many specimens is it possible to have in one aquarium? It

Ole Pedersen

is impossible to answer a question like that, but below are general guidelines to follow (even though there are thousands of exceptions to these).

Fishes with a maximum size of 3 cm — at least 2 litres per fish.

Fishes with a maximum size of 5 cm — at least 5 litres per fish.

Fishes with a maximum size of 7 — 8 cm — at least 10 litres per fish.

Fishes with a maximum size of 15 cm — at least 25 litres per fish.

The maximum size of the Neon Tetra (*Paracheirodon innesi*) is 5 cm. You should have at least 10 individuals in the aquarium; thus you need 10 x 5 litres which corresponds to an aquarium with a minimum size of about 50 x 30 x 35 cm.

Acclimatization

When you buy your fishes they will be packed in a plastic bag in the store. You should treat this bag with care and the faster you get it back home, the better (even though the fish can live for quite some time in the bag). During transportation you should ensure that the bag is not exposed for example to cold or extreme heat, for example by transporting it in an insulated box.

You must ask the salesman about the pH the fishes have been kept in. If you buy them locally it will probably be the same as your tap water. If the pH isn't roughly the same as in your own aquarium the fishes **must** be slowly acclimatized in a quarantine-aquarium (always the best anyway).

If the pH is the same it is possible to put the fishes directly into your aquarium, in the following way.

1. Switch off the lighting
2. Adjust the temperature: Place the bag on the water surface and let it float there. Open the bag and let some water from the aquarium run into it. This should be repeated 3-4 times with an interval of 5-10 minutes. After this time the content of the bag should be approximately 2/3-aquarium water and 1/3 bag water.
3. Let the fishes swim into the aquarium from the bag.
4. Wait an hour before you switch on the lighting.
5. If the aquarium is new, you should not feed the fishes at all during the first day. If there are already fishes in the aquarium, you can feed carefully in the corner opposite to the one where you introduced the new fish.

And now, finally, it is time for you to sit back and enjoy viewing your aquarium. Good luck with your new hobby, I know for sure that you will have just as good a time as I have.

Introduction to fish section

On the following pages I have briefly described about 500 different fish species. You may think that is a lot, but it is in fact just a small fraction of what exists. I have tried to include all of the most common fishes, but also some more unusual species. The fishes that are listed will be enough for most people, but if you want to go further then I recommend that you obtain additional information and read the relevant specialist literature. At the end of this book you will find a page of references to a selection of specialist literature.

It is difficult to group the available fishes in a way that is easy to understand and which at the same time makes it easy to locate particular species. I have made a fairly rough division into groups, and then placed the fishes in alphabetical order within each group. If you nevertheless find it difficult to locate a specific fish, I recommend that you look in the fish index at the end of the book where you will find the scientific names plus some of the trade/hobby names.

The following is a short explanation of the text that appears beneath each fish photo:

Name: The actual scientific name.
Family: The family to which the fish belongs.
Trade name: Earlier/alternative scientific names (synonyms) and popular names (the latter may vary from country to country).

Range: Where in the world you naturally find the fish that is described and sometimes in what habitat.
Temp: Appropriate water temperature.
Max. Size: Approximate maximum size of adult fish.
Water: Suitable pH level (see WATER page 16) in the aquarium.
Aquarium: Minimum length in cm.
Difficulty: On a scale from 1-5. 1 - very hardy aquarium fish. 2 - non-aggressive fish, easy to keep. 3 - suitable as an aquarium fish, but read specialist literature beforehand. 4 - difficult to keep, for specialists only. 5 - not suitable as an aquarium fish.
Comments: This may include a number of different topics, for example: **Food**: First is mentioned whether the species is omnivorous (eats what is offered), herbivorous (requires vegetable food), carnivorous (eats invertebrates and/or fish (the latter are piscivorous)). If omnivorous is mentioned in combination with for example herbivorous, it means that the species is omnivorous but with an emphasis on vegetable food. For additional information see FOOD page 31. Furthermore suitable food for the aquarium is mentioned. **Breeding**: whether the species is a bubblenest builder, egg scatterer, substrate brooder, mouthbrooder, livebearer, or annual fish, etc. For additional information see BREEDING page 37. Pairing fish (keep a pair or a trio), shoaling fish (at least 10), or solitary. **Jumps**: Fishes that can "jump" high and there is a possibility that they will jump out of the aquarium. **Aggressiveness**: It is also mentioned how aggressive a fish is, normally in relation to other fishes in the same group. Some fishes lives in **Brackish water**: Brackish water is everything between fresh water (salinity on 0%) and marine water (salinity on apr. 3.5%), but normally we mean a salinity between 0.5% and 1.5% when we talk about brackish water.

Livebearing Toothcarps (Poeciliidae)

In this group we find many of the most popular aquarium fishes such as guppies, platies, and swordtails. The colourful livebearers we keep in our aquaria bear little resemblance to the livebearers that exist in nature, but are "fancy" (more colourful, longer finnage) forms that have been cultivated in large breeding facilities, principally in Asia but also elsewhere. Their natural habitat extends from North America (eastern United States) and the Caribbean to South America (south to northeastern Argentina and Uruguay). They are hardy fishes that are suited to community aquaria shared with other fishes, and they are therefore usually regarded as "beginners' fishes", but they are also of interest to specialists and in many countries there are special aquarium clubs for people that are interested in livebearers.

They prefer well-lit aquaria with relatively dense vegetation and appreciate some floating plants in a corner. There is no need to detail decor here since the general rules discussed in the first section of this book largely apply in the case of these fishes. Water chemistry is not of major importance, but they prefer slightly alkaline to acid water since the water is alkaline in the natural habitat and in Asia where most of them are bred. The most interesting feature of these fishes is that they give birth to live fry. When the fry are born they are fully developed and immediately swim to the water's surface, fill their swimbladders with air, and begin to search for food. If there is sufficient cover many of the young will survive, otherwise they are likely to be prey for other fishes.

Name: *Anableps anableps.*
Family: Anablepidae.
Trade name: Four-eyed fish.
Range: Venezuela to Brazil.
Temp: 24-28°C. **Max.Size**: 25 cm.
Water: pH 7.5-8.5. **Aquarium**: 160 cm.
Difficulty: 4. **Comments**: Omnivorous. Eats all normal foods. Livebearer. Shoaling fish. Prefer brackish water or marine water. Can be adapted to freshwater, but breeding is contingent on salt in the water. Jumps.

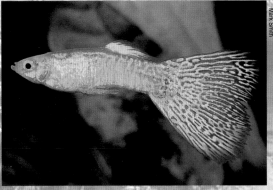

Name: *Poecilia reticulata*.
Family: Poeciliidae.
Trade name: *Lebistes reticulatus*, Guppy.
Range: Central and northern South America.
Temp: 22-28°C.   **Max.Size**: 5,5 cm.
Water: pH 7.0-8.0.   **Aquarium**: 50 cm.
Difficulty: 2-3.   **Comments**: Omnivorous. Eats all normal foods. Livebearer. One of the most popular aquarium fishes. This fish has been inbred to such an extent that this once hardy fish is nowadays sometimes very delicate.

Poecilia sphenops

Poecilia sphenops

Poecilia sphenops

Poecilia sphenops

Name: *Poecilia sphenops.*
Family: Poeciliidae.
Trade name: Black molly, spenops molly.
Range: Central and northern South America.
Temp: 26-28°C (18-28°C in nature).
Max.Size: 10 cm.   **Water**: pH 7.0-8.0.
Aquarium: 60 cm. **Difficulty**: 2-3.
Comments: Omnivorous. Foods with vegetable content necessary. Livebearer. This fish is farm-bred in rather warm and salty water and therefore you may need to add some salt to the aquarium.

Name: *Poecilia velifera.*
Family: Poeciliidae.
Trade name: Sailfin molly.
Range: South-eastern Mexico.
Temp: 25-28°C.   **Max.Size**: 16 cm.
Water: pH 7.0-8.0. **Aquarium**: 100 cm.
Difficulty: 2-3.
Comments: Omnivorous. Foods with vegetable content necessary. Livebearer. This fish is farm-bred in rather warm and salty water and therefore you may need to add some salt to the aquarium.

Poecilia velifera

Poecilia velifera

Name: *Xiphophorus hellerii*.
Family: Poeciliidae.
Trade name: Swordtail.
Range: Mexico, Belize, Honduras.
Temp: 24-28°C.   **Max.Size**: 16 cm.
Water: pH 7.0-8.0. **Aquarium**: 50 cm.
Difficulty: 1-2.
Comments: Omnivorous. Eats all normal foods. Livebearer. Very popular aquarium fish available in many different aquarium strains far from their natural colours. Sometimes are farm-bred fishes delicate.

Name: *Xiphophorus maculatus*.
Family: Poeciliidae.
Trade name: Platy.
Range: Mexico, Guatemala, Honduras.
Temp: 24-28°C.   **Max.Size**: 6 cm.
Water: pH 7.0-8.0. **Aquarium**: 50 cm.
Difficulty: 1-2.
Comments: Omnivorous. Eats all normal foods. Livebearer. Very popular aquarium fish available in many different aquarium strains far from their natural colours. Sometimes are farm-bred fishes delicate.

Carp-like fishes - Cypriniformes

In a scientific context the Cypriniformes are a group that includes a lot of different fishes (more than 2600 species) that don't have much in common, although most are omnivorous (see FOOD) and egg scatterers. Since the Cypriniformes are strictly non-predatory and most are also peaceful, many are good aquarium fishes.

This huge group includes, among others, the popular barbs, the rather odd-looking loaches, the small beautiful rasboras, and the perhaps best-known of all ornamental fishes - the goldfish (*Carassius auratus*). This fish today exists in many different colours and shapes, as a result of selective breeding over many hundreds of years. The goldfish is not only common in our aquaria but also as a pond fish.

Since there are so many different kinds of fishes within this large group, it is pointless to try and provide a general description of their requirements. Instead refer to the general section in the first part of the book, plus, above all, to the text accompanying the photos on the following pages.

Name: *Acantopsis dialuzona*
Family: Cobitidae
Trade name: *Acanthopsis choirorhynchus*, Horse-faced loach.
Range: Southeast Asia.
Temp: 24-28°C   **Max.Size:** 28 cm.
Water: pH 6-6.5.   **Aquarium:** 80 cm.
Difficulty: 3   **Comments**: Omnivorous. Prefer live foods, but eat all normal foods. Peaceful. Cave spawner. Poor swimmers. Bottom-oriented. May bury itself in the substrate (fine sand).

Name: *Balantiocheilus melanopterus*
Family: Cyprinidae
Trade name: Silver shark, tricolor sharkminnow.
Range: Thailand, Malaysia, Indonesia.
Temp: 22-28°C   **Max.Size:** 35 cm.
Water: pH 6-7.5.   **Aquarium:** 120 cm.
Difficulty: 2
Comments: Omnivorous. Eats all normal foods. Peaceful. Shoaling fish. Needs hiding places. Planted aquarium. Jumps.

Name: *Barbus arulius*
Family: Cyprinidae
Trade name: Longfin barb, Aurulius barb.
Range: South and Southeast India.
Temp: 20-25°C   **Max.Size:** 12 cm.
Water: pH 6-7.   **Aquarium:** 80 cm.
Difficulty: 3
Comments: Omnivorous. Eats all normal foods. Needs food with vegetable content. Egg scatterer (among plants). Shoaling fish. Needs hiding places and fine sand. Planted aquarium with an open swimming area.

Name: *Barbus conchonius*
Family: Cyprinidae
Trade name: Rosy barb.
Range: Asia.
Temp: 18-23°C   **Max.Size:** 14 cm.
Water: pH 6-7.5.   **Aquarium:** 80 cm.
Difficulty: 1
Comments: Omnivorous. Eats all normal foods. Adhesive eggs scattered among plants. Shoaling fish. Needs hiding places and fine sand. Planted aquarium with an open swimming area. Doesn't like too warm water.

Name: *Barbus cumingi*
Family: Cyprinidae
Trade name: Cuming´s barb.
Range: Sri Lanka.
Temp: 22-26°C   **Max.Size:** 5 cm.
Water: pH 6.5-7.   **Aquarium:** 60 cm.
Difficulty: 3
Comments: Omnivorous. Eats all normal foods. Adhesive eggs scattered among plants. Shoaling fish. Needs hiding places and fine sand. Planted aquarium with floating plants and an open swimming area.

Name: *Barbus everetti*
Family: Cyprinidae
Trade name: Everett´s barb, Clown barb.
Range: Borneo, Sumatra.
Temp: 24-28°C   **Max.Size:** 15 cm.
Water: pH 6-7.   **Aquarium:** 70 cm.
Difficulty: 3
Comments: Omnivorous. Eats all normal foods. Adhesive eggs scattered among plants. Shoaling fish. Needs hiding places and fine sand. Planted aquarium with floating plants and an open swimming area.

Name: *Barbus filamentosus*
Family: Cyprinidae
Trade name: Blackspot barb.
Range: India, Sri Lanka.
Temp: 20-24°C   **Max.Size:** 12 cm.
Water: pH 6-7.   **Aquarium:** 100 cm.
Difficulty: 3
Comments: Omnivorous. Eats all normal foods. Adhesive eggs scattered among plants. Shoaling fish. Needs hiding places and fine sand. Planted aquarium with floating plants and an open swimming area.

Name: *Barbus nigrofasciatus*
Family: Cyprinidae
Trade name: Black ruby barb, purple-headed barb.
Range: Sri Lanka.
Temp: 22-26°C   **Max.Size:** 6 cm.
Water: pH 6-7.   **Aquarium:** 70 cm.
Difficulty: 2   **Comments**: Omnivorous. Eats all normal foods. Adhesive eggs scattered among plants. Shoaling fish. Needs hiding places and fine sand. Planted aquarium with floating plants and an open swimming area.

Name: *Barbus schwanenfeldii*
Family: Cyprinidae
Trade name: Tinfoil barb, goldfoil barb.
Range: Southeast Asia.
Temp: 22-26°C   **Max.Size:** 34 cm.
Water: pH 6.5-7.   **Aquarium:** 150 cm.
Difficulty: 4
Comments: Omnivorous, but eats small fishes. Eats all normal foods. Shoaling fish. Needs hiding places and fine sand. Planted aquarium with floating plants and an open swimming area. Too big for normal aquarium.

Name: *Barbus semifasciolatus*
Family: Cyprinidae
Trade name: Green barb, Chinese barb.
Range: China.
Temp: 18-25°C   **Max.Size:** 10 cm.
Water: pH 6-7.5.   **Aquarium:** 60 cm.
Difficulty: 1
Comments: Omnivorous. Eats all normal foods. Egg scattered among plants. Shoaling fish. Needs hiding places and fine sand. Planted aquarium with floating plants and an open swimming area. Popular and a good aquarium fish.

Name: *Barbus tetrazona*
Family: Cyprinidae
Trade name: Tiger barb.
Range: Sumatra, Borneo.
Temp: 22-26°C **Max.Size:** 7 cm.
Water: pH 6.5-7.5. **Aquarium:** 80 cm.
Difficulty: 3.
Comments: Omnivorous. Eats all normal foods. Requirements as for other barbs. Sensitive to "white spot disease". Fin-nipper, don't keep this fish together with gouramis and angels. Very popular aquarium fish.

Name: *Barbus titteya*
Family: Cyprinidae
Trade name: Cherry barb.
Range: Sri Lanka.
Temp: 23-26°C **Max.Size:** 5 cm.
Water: pH 6.5-7.5. **Aquarium:** 60 cm.
Difficulty: 1.
Comments: Omnivorous. Eats all normal foods. Egg scattered among plants. Shoaling fish. Requirements as for other barbs. Very popular and good aquarium fish.

Name: *Beaufortia leveretti*
Family: Balitoridae
Trade name: Leverett´s hillstream loach.
Range: China.
Temp: 19-23°C **Max.Size:** 12 cm.
Water: pH 6.5-7.5. **Aquarium:** 100 cm.
Difficulty: 3
Comments: Omnivorous and herbivorous. Eats all normal foods. Breeding behaviour not known, but probably egg scatterer. Peaceful, but somewhat territorial. Oxygen rich water.

Name: *Botia dario*
Family: Cobitidae
Trade name: Bengal loach.
Range: India, Bangladesh, Bhutan.
Temp: 23-26°C **Max.Size:** 15 cm.
Water: pH 6.5-7.5. **Aquarium:** 100 cm.
Difficulty: 4
Comments: Omnivorous and carnivorous. Prefer live foods, but eats all normal foods. Nocturnal and crepuscular. Shoaling fish. Peaceful. Bottom-oriented. May bury itself in the substrate. Needs hiding places and fine sand.

Name: *Botia helodes*
Family: Cobitidae
Trade name: Banded loach, Tiger botia.
Range: Southeast Asia.
Temp: 24-28°C   **Max.Size:** 30 cm.
Water: pH 6.5-7.   **Aquarium:** 120 cm.
Difficulty: 4
Comments: Omnivorous and carnivorous. Piscivorous, eats small fishes. Breeding behaviour not known. Nocturnal. Aggressive. Bottom-oriented. Needs hiding places.

Name: *Botia macracanthus*
Family: Cobitidae
Trade name: Clown loach.
Range: Indonesia.
Temp: 25-30°C   **Max.Size:** 30 cm.
Water: pH 6-7.5.   **Aquarium:** 100 cm.
Difficulty: 3
Comments: Omnivorous. Eats all normal foods, plus aquatic snails. Peaceful. Shoaling fish. More diurnally active than other Botia. Sensitive to "white spot disease". Popular aquarium fish. Needs hiding places and fine sand.

Name: *Botia modesta*
Family: Cobitidae
Trade name: Botia rubripinnis, Orangefin loach.
Range: Southeast Asia.
Temp: 25-30°C   **Max.Size:** 27 cm.
Water: pH 6-7.5.   **Aquarium:** 120 cm.
Difficulty: 3
Comments: Omnivorous and carnivorous. Eats all normal foods. Shoaling fish. Nocturnal and crepuscular. Rather aggressive. Needs hiding places and fine sand

Name: *Botia morleti*
Family: Cobitidae
Trade name: Skunk loach.
Range: Asia.
Temp: 24-30°C   **Max.Size:** 10 cm.
Water: pH 6-7.5.   **Aquarium:** 80 cm.
Difficulty: 3
Comments: Omnivorous. Prefers live and frozen foods. Shoaling fish. Nocturnal and crepuscular. Peaceful. Needs hiding places and fine sand.

Name: *Botia robusta*
Family: Cobitidae
Trade name: Kansu loach.
Range: China.
Temp: 18-25°C   **Max.Size:** 18 cm.
Water: pH 7-8.   **Aquarium:** 120 cm.
Difficulty: 4
Comments: Omnivorous and carnivorous. Eats all normal foods, incl. molluscs. Can eat very small fishes. Nocturnal and crepuscular. Peaceful, but somewhat territorial. Needs hiding places and fine sand.

Name: *Botia sidthimunki*
Family: Cobitidae
Trade name: Dwarf chain loach.
Range: Southeast Asia.
Temp: 24-27°C   **Max.Size:** 5 cm.
Water: pH 6.5-7.5. **Aquarium:** 70 cm.
Difficulty: 3
Comments: Omnivorous and carnivorous. Eats all normal foods. Diurnally active. Shoaling fish. Peaceful. Needs hiding places and fine sand.

Name: *Brachydanio albolineatus*
Family: Cyprinidae
Trade name: Pearl danio.
Range: Southern Asia.
Temp: 20-25°C   **Max.Size:** 7 cm.
Water: pH 6.5-7.5. **Aquarium:** 70 cm.
Difficulty: 1
Comments: Omnivorous and carnivorous. Eats all normal foods. Egg scatterer (among plants). Shoaling fish, but also a pairing fish. Peaceful. Some plants and an open swimming area. Jumps.

Name: *Brachydanio rerio*
Family: Cyprinidae
Trade name: Zebra danio.
Range: Southern Asia.
Temp: 20-25°C   **Max.Size:** 6 cm.
Water: pH 6-7.5.   **Aquarium:** 60 cm.
Difficulty: 1
Comments: Omnivorous and carnivorous. Eats all normal foods. Egg scatterer (among plants). Shoaling fish, but also a pairing fish. Peaceful. Some plants and an open swimming area. Jumps. Very popular aquarium fish.

Carassius auratus

Carassius auratus

Carassius auratus

Carassius auratus

Carassius auratus

Name: *Carassius auratus auratus*
Family: Cyprinidae
Trade name: Goldfish.
Range: Asia.   **Temp:** 10-23°C
Max.Size: 45 cm.   **Water:** pH 6-8.
Aquarium: 120 + ponds.
Difficulty: 2
Comments: Omnivorous. Eats all normal foods, including plants. Egg scatterer. Peaceful. Very popular aquarium and pond fish. This fish has been cultivated for thousands of years and different colour and shape variants occur.

Name: *Chela cachius*
Family: Cyprinidae
Trade name: Cyprinus cachius.
Range: Asia.
Temp: 22-26°C   **Max.Size:** 7 cm.
Water: pH 6.5-7.5. **Aquarium:** 100 cm.
Difficulty: 2
Comments: Omnivorous. Eats all normal foods. Eggs scatterer. Peaceful. Shoaling fish. Planted aquarium with an open swimming area. Dark substrate. Also tolerates brackish water.

Cyprinus carpio

Cyprinus carpio

Cyprinus carpio

Cyprinus carpio

Cyprinus carpio

Name: *Cyprinus carpio* var.
Family: Cyprinidae
Trade name: Koi.
Range: Widespread
Temp: 10-26°C   **Max.Size:** 125 cm.
Water: pH 7-7.5.   **Aquarium:** 200 cm.
Difficulty: 2   **Comments**: Omnivorous. Special koi-foods exist. Egg scatterer. Peaceful. Jumps. Very popular pond fish, but small specimens can also be kept in large aquaria in winter time. This fish has been cultivated for thousands of years and different colour variants occur.

Name: *Crossocheilus siamensis*
Family: Cyprinidae
Trade name: Siamese flying fox, Siamese algae-eater.
Range: Southeast Asia.
Temp: 24-26°C   **Max.Size:** 15 cm.
Water: pH 6.5-7.5.   **Aquarium:** 80 cm.
Difficulty: 2
Comments: Herbivorous. Useful algae-eater, including tuft algae. Eats frozen and vegetable foods. Peaceful against other species, but aggressive towards their own kind. Some hiding places.

Name: *Danio aequipinnatus*
Family: Cyprinidae
Trade name: Giant danio.
Range: Southern Asia.
Temp: 22-24°C   **Max.Size:** 15 cm.
Water: pH 6-7.5.   **Aquarium:** 90 cm.
Difficulty: 2
Comments: Omnivorous. Eats all normal foods. Shoaling fish. Egg scatterer (among plants). Some plants and an open swimming area. Jumps.

Name: *Epalzeorhynchos bicolor*
Family: Cyprinidae
Trade name: Red-tailed black shark, Red-tailed labeo.
Range: Thailand.
Temp: 22-26°C   **Max.Size:** 12 cm.
Water: pH 6.5-7.5. **Aquarium:** 100 cm.
Difficulty: 4.
Comments: Omnivorous and carnivorous. Eats all normal foods. Solitary. Very aggressive towards its own kind. Old specimens aggressive towards all fishes. Needs hiding places.

Name: *Epalzeorhynchos frenatum*
Family: Cyprinidae
Trade name: *Labeo frenatus*, Red-finned shark, Ruby shark.
Range: Thailand, Laos, Cambodia.
Temp: 23-26°C   **Max.Size:** 15 cm.
Water: pH 6-7.5.   **Aquarium:** 100 cm.
Difficulty: 3.
Comments: Omnivorous and carnivorous. Eats all normal foods. Solitary. Somewhat aggressive towards its own kind. Needs hiding places.

Name: *Epalzeorhynchos kalopterus*
Family: Cyprinidae
Trade name: Flying fox.
Range: Southern Asia.
Temp: 24-26°C   **Max.Size:** 16 cm.
Water: pH 6.5-7.   **Aquarium:** 80 cm.
Difficulty: 2.
Comments: Omnivorous and carnivorous. Eats all normal foods. Solitary. Somewhat aggressive towards its own kind. Needs hiding places. Planted aquarium.

61

Name: *Garra pingi pingi*
Family: Cyprinidae
Trade name: Ping´s log sucker.
Range: China.
Temp: 16-28°C   **Max.Size:** 16 cm.
Water: pH 6.5-7.5. **Aquarium:** 80 cm.
Difficulty: 3.
Comments: Omnivorous and carnivorous. Eats all normal foods. Peaceful. Needs clear and moving water. Needs hiding places.

Name: *Gyrinocheilus aymonieri.*
Family: Gyrinocheilidae.
Trade name: Siamese algae-eater, Chinese algae-eater.
Range: Southeast Asia.
Temp: 24-28°C.   **Max.Size**: 28 cm.
Water: pH 6-8.   **Aquarium**: 80 cm.
Difficulty: 2.   **Comments**: Herbivorous. Eats mostly algae but also flake foods and food tablets. Reduced swimbladder. Solitary. Territorial. Small specimens are peaceful and good algae-eaters, adult specimens (larger than 10 cm) are rather aggressive.

Name: *Homaloptera orthogoniata*
Family: Balitoridae
Trade name: Saddled hillstream loach.
Range: Southeast Asia.
Temp: 20-23°C   **Max.Size:** 13 cm.
Water: pH 6.5-7.   **Aquarium:** 100 cm.
Difficulty: 4.
Comments: Omnivorous and herbivorous. Prefers live and frozen foods, but also eats dry foods (with vegetable content). Peaceful, but some aggressions towards its own kind. Breeding behaviour not known. Needs moving water.

Name: *Leptobarbus hoevenii*
Family: Cyprinidae.
Trade name: Red-finned cigar shark.
Range: Southeast Asia.
Temp: 22-26°C   **Max.Size:** 50 cm.
Water: pH 6.5-7.5. **Aquarium:** 150 cm.
Difficulty: 4.
Comments: Omnivorous. Eats all normal foods. Shoaling fish. Some plants and an open swimming area. Needs hiding places. Quite peaceful, but only juveniles are suitable for aquaria.

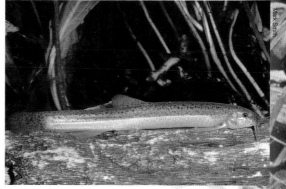

Name: *Luciosoma spilopleura*
Family: Cyprinidae.
Trade name: *Luciosoma setigerum*.
Range: Southeast Asia.
Temp: 23-27°C   **Max.Size:** 25 cm.
Water: pH 5.5-8.   **Aquarium:** 120 cm.
Difficulty: 3.
Comments: Omnivorous. Eats all normal foods. Shoaling fish. Lives close to the surface. Some plants and an open swimming area. Needs hiding places. Jumps.

Name: *Misgurnus anguillicaudatus*
Family: Cobitidae.
Trade name: Chinese weatherfish.
Range: Southern Asia.
Temp: 10-25°C   **Max.Size:** 30 cm.
Water: pH 6.5-7.5. **Aquarium:** 150 cm.
Difficulty: 3.
Comments: Omnivorous. Eats all normal foods. Peaceful. Nocturnal. Bottom-oriented. May burrow in the substrate. Needs hiding places and fine sand.

Name: *Pangio kuhlii*
Family: Cobitidae.
Trade name: Kuhli loach, Coolie loach.
Range: Southern Asia.
Temp: 23-27°C   **Max.Size:** 12 cm.
Water: pH 6-7.   **Aquarium:** 60 cm.
Difficulty: 3.
Comments: Omnivorous and carnivorous. Eats all normal foods. Solitary. Peaceful. Adhesive eggs laid on plants. Crepuscular and nocturnal. May burrow in the substrate. Needs hiding places and fine sand. Dense planting.

Name: *Rasbora borapetensis*
Family: Cyprinidae.
Trade name: Redtail rasbora, blackline rasbora.
Range: Southeast Asia.
Temp: 22-26°C   **Max.Size:** 5 cm.
Water: pH 6.5-7.   **Aquarium:** 50 cm.
Difficulty: 2.   **Comments**: Omnivorous and carnivorous. Eats all normal foods. Adhesive eggs scattered among plants. Peaceful. Shoaling fish. Dense planting with some floating plants and a large open swimming area.

Name: *Rasbora dorsiocellata*
Family: Cyprinidae.
Trade name: Hi-spot rasbora, eye-spot rasbora.
Range: Southeast Asia.
Temp: 20-25°C   **Max.Size:** 6 cm.
Water: pH 6-7.   **Aquarium:** 75 cm.
Difficulty: 2.
Comments: Omnivorous. Eats all normal foods. Adhesive eggs scattered among plants. Peaceful. Shoaling fish. Dense planting with some floating plants and open swimming areas.

Name: *Rasbora espei*
Family: Cyprinidae.
Trade name: Lambchop rasbora.
Range: Thailand.
Temp: 23-27°C   **Max.Size:** 4 cm.
Water: pH 6-6.5.   **Aquarium:** 60 cm.
Difficulty: 3.
Comments: Omnivorous and carnivorous. Eats all normal foods (small foods required). Adhesive eggs scattered among plants. Peaceful. Shoaling fish. Dense planting with some floating plants and open swimming areas.

Name: *Rasbora heteromorpha*
Family: Cyprinidae.
Trade name: Harlequin rasbora.
Range: Southeast Asia.
Temp: 22-25°C   **Max.Size:** 5 cm.
Water: pH 5-7.   **Aquarium:** 50 cm.
Difficulty: 2.
Comments: Omnivorous. Eats all normal foods. Adhesive eggs scattered among plants. Peaceful. Shoaling fish. Dense planting with some floating plants and open swimming areas. Popular aquarium fish.

Name: *Rasbora kalochroma*
Family: Cyprinidae.
Trade name: Clown rasbora, big-spot rasbora.
Range: Southeast Asia.
Temp: 24-28°C   **Max.Size:** 10 cm.
Water: pH 6-6.5.   **Aquarium:** 100 cm.
Difficulty: 3.
Comments: Omnivorous. Eats all normal foods. Adhesive eggs scattered among plants. Peaceful. Somewhat territorial. Dense planting with some floating plants and open swimming areas.

Name: *Rasbora pauciperforata*
Family: Cyprinidae.
Trade name: Redline rasbora, redstripe rasbora.
Range: Southern Asia.
Temp: 23-26°C   **Max.Size:** 7 cm.
Water: pH 5-6.5.   **Aquarium:** 70 cm.
Difficulty: 3.
Comments: Omnivorous. Eats all normal foods. Adhesive eggs scattered among plants. Peaceful. Shoaling fish. Somewhat shy. Dense planting with some floating plants and open swimming areas.

Name: *Rasbora trilineata*
Family: Cyprinidae.
Trade name: Scissortail rasbora, three-line rasbora.
Range: Southeast Asia.
Temp: 23-26°C   **Max.Size:** 13 cm.
Water: pH 6-7.5.   **Aquarium:** 100 cm.
Difficulty: 2
Comments: Omnivorous. Eats all normal foods. Adhesive eggs scattered among plants. Peaceful. Shoaling fish. Dense planting with some floating plants and open swimming areas.

Name: *Sarcocheilichthys sinensis*
Family: Cyprinidae.
Trade name: Amur sucker.
Range: Southern Asia.
Temp: 16-23°C   **Max.Size:** 28 cm.
Water: pH 6.5-7.5. **Aquarium:** 110 cm.
Difficulty: 3
Comments: Carnivorous. Live foods, but accepts also frozen foods. Egg scatterer. Peaceful. Shoaling fish. Some plants and an open swimming area. Needs hiding places. Cool temperature required.

Name: *Tanichthys albonubes*
Family: Cyprinidae.
Trade name: White cloud mountain minnow.
Range: Southern China: White Cloud Mountain.
Temp: 18-23°C   **Max.Size:** 4 cm.
Water: pH 6.5-7.5. **Aquarium:** 60 cm.
Difficulty: 1   **Comments**: Omnivorous. Eats all normal foods. Egg scatterer among plants. Peaceful. Shoaling fish. Dense planting and open swimming areas. Cool temperature required.

CHARACINS (Tetras and their relatives)

The characins are among the best-known and most popular aquarium fishes. Most aquarists will keep neon and/or cardinal tetras at least once. The best-known characins of all are, however, not especially common in the aquarium, namely the piranhas. This because they grow relatively large and are known for their aggressiveness. The piranhas are, however, not especially aggressive in the aquarium, and are actually rather cowardly. Moreover their rapacity in their natural environment has been somewhat exaggerated.

Characins are found mainly in Africa (approx. 200 known species) and in South America (more than 1000 known species). The natural habitat of most characins is clear, oxygen-rich rivers where the water has a neutral or slightly acid. An aquarium with characins should therefore must have efficient filtration to keep the water clean and create surface movement of the water. The pH should preferably not be above 7 and absolutely not over 7.5. Characins are also very often elongate, fast-swimming fishes which do best in a long aquarium. Most people know that characins are shoaling fishes and that for this reason it is best to keep a good number of each species in the aquarium, at least 10 but preferably even more.

The characins also seem to have some kind of signalling system so that they can, for example, warn each other of danger or communicate the presence of food. They are also very sound-sensitive and react very quickly.

In nature most characins are carnivorous or omnivorous, but in the aquarium most are very peaceful and readily eat flake and granulated food. Frozen food is appreciated. Most characins mix well with other fishes with similar water requirements and which are not too rapacious (most characins are small fishes!). Suitable tankmates include, for example, various catfishes (*Corydoras, Otocinclus*, etc.), dwarf cichlids (e.g. *Apistogramma*), and various rasbora species.

When characins breed in their natural environment the majority scatter their eggs among plants and it is therefore a good idea for the aquarium to be densely planted.

Name: *Anostomus anostomus*
Family: Anostomidae
Trade name: Striped headstander.
Range: Amazon, Orinoco, Guyana.
Temp: 22-26°C.   **Max.Size**: 16 cm.
Water: pH 6-7.5   **Aquarium**: 120 cm.
Difficulty: 3
Comments: Herbivorous. Algae eater, but also plant-eaters if fed insufficient vegetable food. Probably egg-scatterer. Best to keep several together. Shoaling fish. Good water movement required (powerful filter).

Name: *Anostomus ternetzi*
Family: Anostomidae
Trade name: Ternetz's headstander.
Range: Brazil.
Temp: 24-26°C.   **Max.Size**: 13 cm.
Water: pH 6-7.5   **Aquarium**: 120 cm.
Difficulty: 2
Comments: Herbivorous. Algae eater, but also plant-eaters if fed insufficient vegetable food. Probably egg-scatterer. Best to keep several together. Shoaling fish. Good water movement required (powerful filter).

Name: *Aphyocharax anisitsi*
Family: Characidae.
Trade name: Bloodfin tetra.
Range: Argentina.
Temp: 20-28°C.   **Max.Size**: 5.5 cm.
Water: pH 6-7.5   **Aquarium**: 60 cm.
Difficulty: 1.
Comments: Omnivorous. Eats all normal foods. Egg-scatterer among plants. Peaceful. Shoaling fish. Planted aquarium. Can be live more than 10 years.

Name: *Aphyocharax paraguayensis*
Family: Characidae.
Trade name: *Hyphessobrycon paraguayensis*, White-spot tetra.
Range: Rio Paraguay basin.
Temp: 22-26°C.   **Max.Size**: 4.5 cm.
Water: pH 6-7   **Aquarium**: 60 cm.
Difficulty: 3.
Comments: Omnivorous. Eats all normal foods. Egg-scatterer among plants. Peaceful. Shoaling fish. Planted aquarium. Somewhat sensitive.

Name: *Aphyocharax rathbuni*
Family: Characidae.
Trade name: Redflank bloodfin.
Range: Rio Paraguay basin.
Temp: 20-25°C.   **Max.Size**: 4.5 cm.
Water: pH 6.5-7.5 **Aquarium**: 80 cm.
Difficulty: 2.
Comments: Omnivorous. Eats all normal foods. Egg-scatterer among plants. Peaceful. Shoaling fish. Planted aquarium.

Name: *Arnoldichthys spilopterus*
Family: Alestiidae.
Trade name: Niger tetra, Arnold´s tetra.
Range: Lagos to the Niger delta.
Temp: 23-27°C.   **Max.Size**: 9.5 cm.
Water: pH 6-7.5   **Aquarium**: 100 cm.
Difficulty: 3.
Comments: Omnivorous. Prefers live food, but eats all normal foods. Egg-scatterer among plants. Peaceful. Shoaling fish. Several hiding-places. Planted aquarium. Fine-grained sand substrate.

Name: *Astyanax fasciatus mexicanus*
Family: Characidae.
Trade name: Blind cave tetra.
Range: Texas to Panama.
Temp: 20-25°C.   **Max.Size**: 11 cm.
Water: pH 6.5-9.   **Aquarium**: 80 cm.
Difficulty: 2.
Comments: Omnivorous. Eats all normal foods. Egg-scatterer. Peaceful. Shoaling fish. Although this fish is blind, it can be kept in a normal community aquarium.

Name: *Bathyaethiops caudomaculatus*
Family: Alestiidae.
Trade name: African moon tetra.
Range: Zaire, Cameroon.
Temp: 23-26°C.   **Max.Size**: 8 cm.
Water: pH 6.5-7.5 **Aquarium**: 100 cm.
Difficulty: 3.
Comments: Omnivorous. Prefers live food, but eats all normal foods. Egg-scatterer among plants. Peaceful. Shoaling fish. Several hiding-places. Planted aquarium. Fine grained sand substrate.

Name: *Belonophago tinanti*
Family: Citharinidae.
Trade name: Needle fin-eater.
Range: Congo basin, Ubangi river.
Temp: 23-26°C.   **Max.Size**: 15 cm.
Water: pH 6-7   **Aquarium**: 150 cm.
Difficulty: 4.
Comments: Carnivorous. Piscivorous. Insect larvae, small fishes and fins, sometimes frozen foods. Probably an egg-scatterer. Not for a community aquarium. Planted aquarium. Needs hiding places.

Name: *Boehlkea fredcochui*
Family: Characidae.
Trade name: Cochu's blue tetra.
Range: Upper Amazon river basin.
Temp: 23-26°C.   **Max.Size**: 5 cm.
Water: pH 6-7.5   **Aquarium**: 60 cm.
Difficulty: 3.
Comments: Omnivorous. Eats all normal foods. Egg-scatterer among plants. Peaceful. Shoaling fish. Oxygen-rich water. Sensitive to transportation.

Name: *Boulengerella lateristriga*
Family: Ctenoluciidae.
Trade name: Striped pike-characin.
Range: Brazil, Venezuela.
Temp: 23-26°C.   **Max.Size**: 40 cm.
Water: pH 6-7   **Aquarium**: 250 cm.
Difficulty: 4.
Comments: Carnivorous. Piscivorous. Needs live foods. Shy. Oxygen-rich water. Very sensitive to bad water quality.

Name: *Boulengerella maculata*
Family: Ctenoluciidae.
Trade name: Spotted pike-characin.
Range: Rios Amazon, Tocantins, and Orinoco.
Temp: 23-26°C.   **Max.Size**: 40 cm.
Water: pH 6-7.5   **Aquarium**: 350 cm.
Difficulty: 5.
Comments: Carnivorous. Piscivorous. Needs live foods. Shy. Oxygen-rich water. Very sensitive to bad water quality. Too big for most aquaria.

69

Name: *Brycon melanopterus*
Family: Characidae.
Trade name: Sickle-band Brycon.
Range: Amazon-basin.
Temp: 23-26°C.   **Max.Size**: 18 cm.
Water: pH 6-7.5   **Aquarium**: 200 cm.
Difficulty: 3.
Comments: Omnivorous. Young fishes eat all normal foods. Full-grown specimens need large live food. Shoaling fish. Egg-scatterer among plants. Peaceful, but large specimens eat small fishes. Oxygen-rich water.

Name: *Carnegiella marthae*
Family: Gasteropelecidae.
Trade name: Black-winged hatchetfish.
Range: Venezuela, Brazil.
Temp: 24-27°C.   **Max.Size**: 3.5 cm.
Water: pH 5.5-6.5 **Aquarium**: 60 cm.
Difficulty: 4.
Comments: Carnivorous. Small live and frozen foods, but also eats dry food. Peaceful. Shoaling fish. Shy. Egg-scatterer among plants. Needs oxygen-rich water. Very sensitive, especially susceptible to white spot disease. Jumps.

Name: *Carnegiella strigata*
Family: Gasteropelecidae.
Trade name: Marbled hatchetfish.
Range: Amazon basin, the Guianas.
Temp: 24-27°C.   **Max.Size**: 4 cm.
Water: pH 5.5-7.   **Aquarium**: 60 cm.
Difficulty: 3.
Comments: Carnivorous. Small live and frozen foods, but also eats dry food. Peaceful. Shoaling fish. Shy. Egg-scatterer among plants. Needs oxygen rich water. Very sensitive, especially susceptible to white spot disease. Jumps.

Name: *Chalceus erythrurus*
Family: Characidae.
Trade name: Yellow-finned Chalceus.
Range: Amazonas area.
Temp: 23-26°C.   **Max.Size**: 25 cm.
Water: pH 6-7.   **Aquarium**: 150 cm.
Difficulty: 4.
Comments: Carnivorous. Piscivorous — eats small fishes. Eats all normal foods. Shoaling fish. Jumps. Good to eat.

Name: *Chilodus punctatus*
Family: Anostomidae.
Trade name: Spotted headstander.
Range: Guyana, Venezuela, Brazil.
Temp: 23-28°C.   **Max.Size**: 10 cm.
Water: pH 6-7.   **Aquarium**: 100 cm.
Difficulty: 3.
Comments: Omnivorous. Algae-eater. Eats all normal foods. Egg-scatterer among plants. Peaceful. Sometimes shy.

Name: *Colossoma brachypomus*
Family: Characidae.
Trade name: Silver pacu, pacu.
Range: Amazonas and Orinoco basin.
Temp: 23-28°C.   **Max.Size**: 45 cm.
Water: pH 5-7.   **Aquarium**: 300 cm.
Difficulty: 5.
Comments: Omnivorous. Plant eater. Not possible to keep in a planted aquarium. Eats plants, fruits, etc. Juveniles eat all normal foods. Shoaling fish. Needs hiding-places. Too big for normal aquaria.

Name: *Colossoma macropomum*
Family: Characidae.
Trade name: Black pacu.
Range: Amazonas and Orinoco basin.
Temp: 23-28°C.   **Max.Size**: 95 cm.
Water: pH 5-8.   **Aquarium**: 300 cm.
Difficulty: 5.
Comments: Omnivorous. Plant eater. Not possible to keep in a planted aquarium. Eats vegetable foods. Juveniles eat all normal foods. Shoaling fish. Needs hiding-places. Too big for normal aquaria.

Name: *Copella arnoldi*
Family: Lebiasinidae.
Trade name: Splash tetra.
Range: Lower Amazon, Guianas.
Temp: 24-28°C.   **Max.Size**: 8 cm.
Water: pH 6-7.5.   **Aquarium**: 80 cm.
Difficulty: 2.
Comments: Omnivorous. Eats all normal foods. Attaches eggs to the underside of plant leaves above the water, or on the aquarium cover glass. Peaceful. Do not keep together with lively shoaling fishes. Jumps.

Name: *Copella nattereri*
Family: Lebiasinidae.
Trade name: Spotted tetra.
Range: Lower Amazon and Orinoco basin.
Temp: 23-28°C.   **Max.Size**: 6 cm.
Water: pH 6-7.   **Aquarium**: 60 cm.
Difficulty: 3.
Comments: Omnivorous. Eats all normal foods. Attaches eggs to plant leaves. Peaceful. Do not keep together with lively shoaling fishes. Jumps.

Name: *Distichodus sexfasciatus*
Family: Citharinidae.
Trade name: Sixbarred Distichodus.
Range: Zaire, Angola.
Temp: 23-26°C.   **Max.Size**: 75 cm.
Water: pH 6-7.5.   **Aquarium**: 300 cm.
Difficulty: 5.
Comments: Herbivorous. Plant eater. Not possible to keep in planted aquariums. Needs vegetable food. Egg-scatterer. Shoaling fish. Old fishes are grey-yellow with grey fins. Peaceful, but too big for normal aquaria.

Name: *Exodon paradoxus*
Family: Characidae.
Trade name: Bucktooth tetra.
Range: Amazon basin, Guyana.
Temp: 23-26°C.   **Max.Size**: 15 cm.
Water: pH 6-7.   **Aquarium**: 120 cm.
Difficulty: 4.
Comments: Carnivorous. Piscivorous — eats smaller fishes. Eats all normal foods. Egg-scatterer among plants. Shoaling fish — minimum 15 individuals. Jumps.

Name: *Gasteropelecus sternicla*
Family: Gasteropelecidae.
Trade name: Common hatchetfish.
Range: Brazil, Guyana, Surinam.
Temp: 23-26°C.   **Max.Size**: 6.5 cm.
Water: pH 6.5-7.5. **Aquarium**: 80 cm.
Difficulty: 3.
Comments: Carnivorous. Small live and frozen foods, but also eats dry food. Peaceful. Shoaling fish. Shy. Egg-scatterer among plants. Needs oxygen-rich water. Sensitive, especially susceptible to white spot disease. Jumps.

Name: *Gymnocorymbus ternetzi*
Family: Characidae.
Trade name: Black tetra, Black widow.
Range: Bolivia, Brazil, Argentina.
Temp: 21-26°C.　**Max.Size**: 6 cm.
Water: pH 6.5-7.5. **Aquarium**: 60 cm.
Difficulty: 1.
Comments: Omnivorous. Eats all normal foods. Peaceful. Shoaling fish. Egg-scatterer among plants. Common aquarium fish. Old fishes lose the beautiful black colour.

Name: *Hasemania nana*
Family: Characidae.
Trade name: Silver-tip tetra.
Range: Southeast Brazil.
Temp: 23-27°C.　**Max.Size**: 5 cm.
Water: pH 6-7.5.　**Aquarium**: 60 cm.
Difficulty: 1.
Comments: Omnivorous. Eats all normal foods. Peaceful. Shoaling fish. Egg-scatterer among plants. Common aquarium fish.

Name: *Hemigrammus bleheri*
Family: Characidae.
Trade name: Rummy nose, firehead tetra.
Range: Colombia, Brazil.
Temp: 23-26°C.　**Max.Size**: 4.5 cm.
Water: pH 5-6.5.　**Aquarium**: 90 cm.
Difficulty: 3.
Comments: Omnivorous. Eats all normal foods. Peaceful. Shoaling fish. Egg-scatterer among plants. Somewhat sensitive

Name: *Hemigrammus caudovittatus*
Family: Characidae.
Trade name: Buenos Aires tetra.
Range: Argentina.
Temp: 20-26°C.　**Max.Size**: 7 cm.
Water: pH 6-8.　**Aquarium**: 100 cm.
Difficulty: 2.
Comments: Omnivorous. Plant eater. Eats all normal foods. Egg-scatterer among plants. Peaceful. Shoaling fish. Good aquarium fish in aquarium without plants.

Name: *Hemigrammus erythrozonus*
Family: Characidae.
Trade name: Glowlight tetra.
Range: Guyana: Essequibo river basin..
Temp: 24-27°C.   **Max.Size**: 4 cm.
Water: pH 6-7.5.   **Aquarium**: 60 cm.
Difficulty: 2.
Comments: Omnivorous. Eats all normal foods. Egg-scatterer among plants. Peaceful. Shoaling fish. Common aquarium fish.

Name: *Hemigrammus hyanuary*
Family: Characidae.
Trade name: Costello tetra, green neon, January tetra.
Range: Colombia, Peru, Brazil.
Temp: 24-27°C.   **Max.Size**: 4 cm.
Water: pH 6-7.5.   **Aquarium**: 60 cm.
Difficulty: 2.
Comments: Omnivorous. Eats all normal foods. Egg-scatterer among plants. Peaceful. Shoaling fish.

Name: *Hemigrammus ocellifer*
Family: Characidae.
Trade name: Head-and-tail-light tetra.
Range: Guianas and Amazon basin.
Temp: 24-27°C.   **Max.Size**: 4.5 cm.
Water: pH 6-7.5.   **Aquarium**: 60 cm.
Difficulty: 1.
Comments: Omnivorous. Eats all normal foods. Egg-scatterer among plants. Peaceful. Shoaling fish. Easy to breed.

Name: *Hemigrammus pulcher*
Family: Characidae.
Trade name: Pretty tetra, garnet tetra.
Range: Upper Amazon river basin.
Temp: 24-27°C.   **Max.Size**: 4.5 cm.
Water: pH 5.5-6.5. **Aquarium**: 60 cm.
Difficulty: 2.
Comments: Omnivorous. Eats all normal foods. Egg-scatterer among plants. Peaceful. Shoaling fish.

Name: *Hemigrammus rodwayi*
Family: Characidae.
Trade name: Golden tetra.
Range: Guyana, Peru, Brazil, French Guiana.
Temp: 24-27°C.   **Max.Size**: 5.5 cm.
Water: pH 6-7.   **Aquarium**: 60 cm.
Difficulty: 4.
Comments: Omnivorous. Eats all normal foods. Egg-scatterer among plants. Peaceful. Shoaling fish. Wild fishes are metallic gold because an infection (not contagious). Captive-bred fishes don't have this colour.

Name: *Hemigrammus ulreyi*
Family: Characidae.
Trade name: Ulrey's tetra.
Range: Rio Paraguay basin.
Temp: 24-27°C.   **Max.Size**: 5 cm.
Water: pH 6-7.   **Aquarium**: 75 cm.
Difficulty: 2.
Comments: Omnivorous. Eats all normal foods. Egg-scatterer among plants. Peaceful. Shoaling fish.

Name: *Hyphessobrycon callistus*
Family: Characidae.
Trade name: Serpae tetra.
Range: Paraguay basin and Paraná.
Temp: 22-26°C.   **Max.Size**: 4 cm.
Water: pH 6-7.5.   **Aquarium**: 80 cm.
Difficulty: 3.
Comments: Omnivorous. Eats all normal foods. Egg-scatterer among plants. Peaceful. Shoaling fish. If they don't get enough food they may attack other fishes in a shoal, as do piranhas.

Name: *Hyphessobrycon erythrostigma*
Family: Characidae.
Trade name: Bleeding heart tetra.
Range: Peru, Colombia, Brazil.
Temp: 24-27°C.   **Max.Size**: 8 cm.
Water: pH 5.5-7.   **Aquarium**: 100 cm.
Difficulty: 2.
Comments: Omnivorous. Eats all normal foods. Egg-scatterer among plants. Peaceful. Shoaling fish. Popular aquarium fish, but not bred commercially.

Name: *Hyphessobrycon flammeus*
Family: Characidae.
Trade name: Flame tetra.
Range: Brazil.
Temp: 23-27°C.   **Max.Size**: 4,5 cm.
Water: pH 6-7.5.   **Aquarium**: 60 cm.
Difficulty: 1.
Comments: Omnivorous. Eats all normal foods. Egg-scatterer among plants. Peaceful. Shoaling fish. Better colours in muted light.

Name: *Hyphessobrycon griemi*
Family: Characidae.
Trade name: Gold-spotted tetra.
Range: Southeastern Brazil.
Temp: 23-27°C.   **Max.Size**: 3.5 cm.
Water: pH 6-7.5.   **Aquarium**: 60 cm.
Difficulty: 2.
Comments: Omnivorous. Eats all normal foods. Egg-scatterer among plants. Peaceful. Shoaling fish.

Name: *Hyphessobrycon haraldschultzi*
Family: Characidae.
Trade name: Schultz´s tetra.
Range: Brazil, Colombia.
Temp: 23-26°C.   **Max.Size**: 4 cm.
Water: pH 6-6.5.   **Aquarium**: 60 cm.
Difficulty: 3.
Comments: Omnivorous. Eats all normal foods. Egg-scatterer among plants. Peaceful. Shoaling fish. Soft and acid water is necessary.

Name: *Hyphessobrycon herbertaxelrodi*
Family: Characidae.
Trade name: Black neon tetra.
Range: Brazil: Taquari river.
Temp: 23-27°C.   **Max.Size**: 4 cm.
Water: pH 6-7.5.   **Aquarium**: 60 cm.
Difficulty: 2.
Comments: Omnivorous. Eats all normal foods. Egg-scatterer among plants. Peaceful. Shoaling fish. Common aquarium fish.

Name: *Hyphessobrycon heterorhabdus*
Family: Characidae.
Trade name: Flag tetra.
Range: Amazonas area.
Temp: 23-27°C.   **Max.Size**: 4,5 cm.
Water: pH 6-7.5.   **Aquarium**: 60 cm.
Difficulty: 2.
Comments: Omnivorous. Eats all normal foods. Egg-scatterer among plants. Peaceful. Shoaling fish.

Name: *Hyphessobrycon loretoensis*
Family: Characidae.
Trade name: Loreto tetra.
Range: Peru, Brazil, Colombia.
Temp: 23-26°C.   **Max.Size**: 4 cm.
Water: pH 6-7.5.   **Aquarium**: 60 cm.
Difficulty: 3.
Comments: Omnivorous. Eats all normal foods. Egg-scatterer among plants. Peaceful. Shoaling fish. Somewhat sensitive.

Name: *Hyphessobrycon pulchripinnis*
Family: Characidae.
Trade name: Lemon tetra.
Range: Brazil: Amazon basin.
Temp: 23-26°C.   **Max.Size**: 4 cm.
Water: pH 6-7.5.   **Aquarium**: 60 cm.
Difficulty: 2.
Comments: Carnivorous and omnivorous. Eats all normal foods. Egg-scatterer among plants. Peaceful. Shoaling fish. Somewhat shy.

Name: *Hyphessobrycon pyrrhonotus*
Family: Characidae.
Trade name: Red-back bleeding-heart tetra.
Range: Brazil: Rio Negro.
Temp: 23-26°C.   **Max.Size**: 6 cm.
Water: pH 6-7.5.   **Aquarium**: 80 cm.
Difficulty: 3.
Comments: Carnivorous. Eats all normal foods. Egg-scatterer among plants. Peaceful. Shoaling fish. Better colours in muted light.

Name: *Hyphessobrycon rosaceus*
Family: Characidae.
Trade name: Rosy tetra.
Range: Guyana, Brazil, Surinam, lower Amazon River basin.
Temp: 24-27°C. **Max.Size**: 4 cm.
Water: pH 6-7.5. **Aquarium**: 60 cm.
Difficulty: 1.
Comments: Omnivorous. Eats all normal foods. Egg-scatterer among plants. Peaceful. Shoaling fish. The "rosy" colour varies according to habitat.

Name: *Hyphessobrycon socolofi*
Family: Characidae.
Trade name: Spotfin tetra.
Range: Brazil: Rio Negro.
Temp: 23-26°C. **Max.Size**: 4.5 cm.
Water: pH 6-7. **Aquarium**: 60 cm.
Difficulty: 3.
Comments: Omnivorous and carnivorous. Eats all normal foods. Egg-scatterer among plants. Peaceful. Shoaling fish. Better colours in muted light.

Name: *Inpaichthys kerri*
Family: Characidae.
Trade name: Blue emperor, Royal tetra.
Range: Brazil.
Temp: 24-27°C. **Max.Size**: 4 cm.
Water: pH 6-7.5. **Aquarium**: 60 cm.
Difficulty: 2.
Comments: Omnivorous. Eats all normal foods. Egg-scatterer among plants. Peaceful. Shoaling fish. Better colours in muted light. Only males are bluish.

Name: *Leporinus arcus*
Family: Anostomidae.
Trade name: Lipstick Leporinus.
Range: Venezuela, Guianas.
Temp: 23-26°C. **Max.Size**: 40 cm.
Water: pH 6-7.5. **Aquarium**: 200 cm.
Difficulty: 4.
Comments: Herbivorous. Needs food with vegetable content. Not possible in a planted aquarium. Sometimes aggressive towards its own kind. Jumps. Good water movement required (powerful filtration).

Name: *Leporinus desmotes*
Family: Anostomidae.
Trade name: Trunk Leporinus.
Range: Guyana, Amazonas area.
Temp: 23-26°C. **Max.Size**: 18 cm.
Water: pH 6-7.5. **Aquarium**: 150 cm.
Difficulty: 4.
Comments: Herbivorous. Needs food with vegetable content. Not possible in a planted aquarium. Shoaling fish. Peaceful. Jumps. Good water movement required (powerful filtration).

Name: *Leporinus fasciatus*
Family: Anostomidae.
Trade name: Banded Leporinus.
Range: Northern and central South America.
Temp: 23-26°C. **Max.Size**: 30 cm.
Water: pH 6-7.5. **Aquarium**: 200 cm.
Difficulty: 4.
Comments: Herbivorous. Needs foods with vegetable content. Not possible in a planted aquarium. Shoaling fish. Sometimes aggressive towards its own kind. Jumps. Good water movement required (powerful filtration).

Name: *Megalamphodus megalopterus*
Family: Characidae.
Trade name: Black phantom tetra.
Range: Brazil, Bolivia.
Temp: 23-28°C. **Max.Size**: 4.5 cm.
Water: pH 6-7.5. **Aquarium**: 70 cm.
Difficulty: 2.
Comments: Omnivorous and carnivorous. Eats all normal foods. Egg-scatterer among plants. Peaceful. Shoaling fish.

Name: *Megalamphodus sweglesi*
Family: Characidae.
Trade name: Red phantom tetra.
Range: Colombia.
Temp: 21-23°C. **Max.Size**: 4 cm.
Water: pH 5.5-7. **Aquarium**: 70 cm.
Difficulty: 3.
Comments: Omnivorous and carnivorous. Needs live food. Peaceful. Shoaling fish. Egg-scatterer. Not too warm water. Somewhat sensitive.

Name: *Metynnis argenteus*
Family: Serrasalmidae.
Trade name: Silver dollar, silver Metynnis.
Range: South of the lower Amazon.
Temp: 23-28°C.   **Max.Size**: 14 cm.
Water: pH 6-7.   **Aquarium**: 150 cm.
Difficulty: 3.
Comments: Herbivorous. Feed with vegetable foods. Egg-scatterer among plants. Peaceful. Shoaling fish. Oxygen-rich water. Needs hiding-places.

Name: *Moenkhausia pittieri*
Family: Characidae.
Trade name: Diamond tetra.
Range: Venezuela: Lake Valencia.
Temp: 23-28°C.   **Max.Size**: 6 cm.
Water: pH 6-7.   **Aquarium**: 80 cm.
Difficulty: 3.
Comments: Omnivorous and carnivorous. Needs live food. Peaceful. Shoaling fish. Egg-scatterer. Muted light.

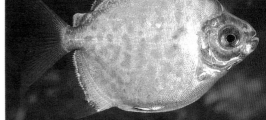

Name: *Moenkhausia sanctaefilomenae*
Family: Characidae.
Trade name: Red-eye tetra.
Range: Brazil, Paraguay.
Temp: 23-26°C.   **Max.Size**: 6 cm.
Water: pH 6-7.5.   **Aquarium**: 80 cm.
Difficulty: 1.
Comments: Omnivorous and carnivorous. Needs live food. Peaceful. Shoaling fish. Egg-scatterer among plants. Common aquarium fish.

Name: *Myleus pacu* (juvenile)
Family: Characidae.
Trade name: Brown giant pacu.
Range: Guianas, Amazonas area.
Temp: 23-28°C.   **Max.Size**: 50 cm.
Water: pH 6.5-7.5. **Aquarium**: 300 cm.
Difficulty: 5.
Comments: Herbivorous. Feed with vegetable foods. Egg-scatterer among plants. Peaceful. Shoaling fish. Needs hiding-places.

Name: *Myleus rubripinnis*
Family: Characidae.
Trade name: Red-hook.
Range: Venezuela, Surinam, Guianas, Peru.
Temp: 23-28°C.　　**Max.Size**: 30 cm.
Water: pH 5.5-7.　　**Aquarium**: 200 cm.
Difficulty: 4.
Comments: Omnivorous. Plant eater. Feed with vegetable foods, but eats all normal foods. Egg-scatterer among plants. Peaceful. Shoaling fish. Oxygen rich water. Needs hiding-places.

Name: *Nannaethiops unitaeniatus*
Family: Citharinidae.
Trade name: One-line tetra.
Range: Zaire to the Niger.
Temp: 23-26°C.　　**Max.Size**: 7 cm.
Water: pH 6.5-7.5.　**Aquarium**: 80 cm.
Difficulty: 3.
Comments: Carnivorous. Eats live and frozen foods. Egg-scatterer among plants. Peaceful. Shoaling fish. Shy. Preferably not mixed with other fishes.

Name: *Nannobrycon eques*
Family: Lebiasinidae.
Trade name: Brown pencilfish, hockey-stick pencilfish.
Range: Colombia, Brazil, Guyana.
Temp: 24-27°C.　　**Max.Size**: 5 cm.
Water: pH 5-6.5.　　**Aquarium**: 80 cm.
Difficulty: 3.
Comments: Carnivorous. Small live or frozen foods, sometimes also eats dry food. Peaceful. Shoaling fish. Egg-scatterer among plants. Needs hiding-places. Somewhat sensitive.

Name: *Nannobrycon unifasciatus*
Family: Lebiasinidae.
Trade name: One-lined pencilfish.
Range: Colombia, Brazil, Guyana.
Temp: 25-27°C.　　**Max.Size**: 7 cm.
Water: pH 5.5-7.　**Aquarium**: 80 cm.
Difficulty: 3.
Comments: Carnivorous. Small live or frozen foods, sometimes also eats dry food. Peaceful. Shoaling fish. Egg-scatterer among plants. Densely planted aquarium. Needs hiding-places. Somewhat sensitive.

81

Name: *Nannostomus espei*
Family: Lebiasinidae.
Trade name: Barred pencilfish, Espe's pencilfish.
Range: Guyana.
Temp: 23-26°C. **Max.Size**: 4 cm.
Water: pH 6-7. **Aquarium**: 60 cm.
Difficulty: 4.
Comments: Omnivorous. Small live or frozen foods, sometimes also eats dry food. Peaceful. Shoaling fish. Adhesive spawner, on plants. Densely planted aquarium. Needs hiding-places. Somewhat sensitive.

Name: *Nannostomus harrisoni*
Family: Lebiasinidae.
Trade name: Blackstripe pencilfish, Harrison´s pencilfish.
Range: Guyana.
Temp: 23-28°C. **Max.Size**: 6 cm.
Water: pH 6-7. **Aquarium**: 80 cm.
Difficulty: 3.
Comments: Omnivorous. Small live or frozen foods, sometimes also eats dry food. Peaceful. Shoaling fish. Egg-scatterer among plants. Densely planted aquarium. Needs hiding-places. Somewhat sensitive.

Name: *Nannostomus marginatus*
Family: Lebiasinidae.
Trade name: Dwarf pencilfish.
Range: Guyana, Colombia, Surinam.
Temp: 24-26°C. **Max.Size**: 3.5 cm.
Water: pH 6-7.5. **Aquarium**: 50 cm.
Difficulty: 3.
Comments: Omnivorous. Small live or frozen foods, sometimes also eats dry food. Peaceful. Shoaling fish. Egg-scatterer among plants. Densely planted aquarium. Needs hiding-places. Somewhat sensitive.

Name: *Nematobrycon palmeri*
Family: Characidae.
Trade name: Emperor tetra.
Range: Colombia.
Temp: 23-26°C. **Max.Size**: 5,5 cm.
Water: pH 5.5-7.5. **Aquarium**: 75 cm.
Difficulty: 3.
Comments: Omnivorous. Needs live foods, but also eats dry food. Peaceful. Shoaling fish. Egg-scatterer among plants. Do not keep with excessively lively fishes. Somewhat sensitive.

Name: *Neolebias ansorgii*
Family: Citharinidae.
Range: Nigeria, Zaire, Cameroon, Gabon.
Temp: 23-28°C.   **Max.Size**: 3,5 cm.
Water: pH 5.5-6.5. **Aquarium**: 50 cm.
Difficulty: 4.
Comments: Carnivorous and omnivorous. Live food, but also frozen and dry foods. Egg-scatterer in the bottom substrate (peat fibres or Java moss). Peaceful. Planted aquarium. Rather sensitive. Shy.

Name: *Neolebias trewavasae*
Family: Citharinidae.
Range: Congo and Nile basins.
Temp: 23-26°C.   **Max.Size**: 5 cm.
Water: pH 5.5-6.5. **Aquarium**: 60 cm.
Difficulty: 3.
Comments: Carnivorous and omnivorous. Live foods, but also frozen and dry foods. Egg-scatterer in the bottom substrate (peat fibres or Java moss). Peaceful. Planted aquarium. Rather sensitive. Shy.

Name: *Paracheirodon axelrodi*
Family: Characidae.
Trade name: Cardinal tetra.
Range: Venezuela, Colombia, Brazil.
Temp: 23-26°C.   **Max.Size**: 5 cm.
Water: pH 5.5-7.   **Aquarium**: 60 cm.
Difficulty: 3.
Comments: Omnivorous and carnivorous. Eats all normal foods. Peaceful. Shoaling fish. Egg-scatterer among plants. Rather sensitive (Neon disease). Very popular aquarium fish. Most of the fishes in the trade are wild caught.

Name: *Paracheirodon innesi*
Family: Characidae.
Trade name: Neon tetra.
Range: Peru, Colombia, Brazil.
Temp: 22-26°C.   **Max.Size**: 5 cm.
Water: pH 5.5-7.   **Aquarium**: 50 cm.
Difficulty: 2.
Comments: Carnivorous and omnivorous. Eats all normal foods. Shoaling fish. Very peaceful. Egg-scatterer among plants. Probably the most popular aquarium fish.

Name: *Paracheirodon simulans*
Family: Characidae.
Trade name: False neon tetra.
Range: Brazil: Rio Negro, Colombia, Venezuela.
Temp: 23-26°C.   **Max.Size**: 4 cm.
Water: pH 5.5-6.5. **Aquarium**: 60 cm.
Difficulty: 3.
Comments: Carnivorous and omnivorous. Live foods, but also eats all normal foods. Shoaling fish. Very peaceful. Egg-scatterer among plants. Rather sensitive.

Name: *Phenacogrammus interruptus*
Family: Alestiidae.
Trade name: Congo tetra.
Range: Congo basin.
Temp: 23-27°C.   **Max.Size**: 8 cm.
Water: pH 6-7.5.   **Aquarium**: 100 cm.
Difficulty: 2.
Comments: Omnivorous and carnivorous. Prefers live food, but eats all normal foods. Egg-scatterer among plants. Peaceful. Shoaling fish. Several hiding-places. Planted aquarium.

Name: *Pristella maxillaris*
Family: Characidae.
Trade name: X-ray tetra.
Range: Brazil, Venezuela, Guianas.
Temp: 24-27°C.   **Max.Size**: 4,5 cm.
Water: pH 6-7.5.   **Aquarium**: 60 cm.
Difficulty: 1.
Comments: Carnivorous and omnivorous. Eats all normal foods. Egg-scatterer among plants. Shoaling fish. Very peaceful.

Name: *Pseudocorynopoma doriae*
Family: Characidae.
Trade name: Dragon-fin tetra.
Range: Brazil: La Plata region.
Temp: 20-25°C.   **Max.Size**: 8 cm.
Water: pH 6.5-7.5. **Aquarium**: 80 cm.
Difficulty: 1.
Comments: Omnivorous. Eats all normal foods. Shoaling fish. Egg-scatterer among plants. Needs oxygen-rich water. Peaceful.

Name: *Pygocentrus nattereri*
Family: Cahracidae.
Trade name: *Serrasalmus nattereri*, Piranha.
Range: Guyana.
Temp: 23-28°C.   **Max.Size**: 35 cm.
Water: pH 5.5-7.5. **Aquarium**: 200 cm.
Difficulty: 4.
Comments: Carnivorous. Piscivorous. Eats frozen food, fillet of fishes, sometimes also pellets. Egg-scatterer among plants. Shoaling fish. Can be dangerous in the wild, often rather shy in the aquariums (stress), but be careful.

Name: *Thayeria boehlkei*
Family: Characidae.
Trade name: Penguin fish.
Range: Brazil, Peru.
Temp: 23-28°C.   **Max.Size**: 6 cm.
Water: pH 6-7.5.   **Aquarium**: 70 cm.
Difficulty: 2.
Comments: Carnivorous and omnivorous. Eats all normal foods. Egg-scatterer among plants. Shoaling fish. Very peaceful. Sensitive to bad water quality.

Name: *Thayeria obliqua*
Family: Characidae.
Trade name: Penguin fish.
Range: Brazil: Amazon basin.
Temp: 23-28°C.   **Max.Size**: 8 cm.
Water: pH 6-7.   **Aquarium**: 80 cm.
Difficulty: 3.
Comments: Carnivorous and omnivorous. Eats all normal foods. Egg-scatterer among plants. Shoaling fish. Very peaceful. Sensitive to bad water quality.

Name: *Triportheus rotundatus*
Family: Characidae.
Trade name: Black-winged hatchetfish.
Range: Amazon basin, Guianas and Venezuela.
Temp: 24-27°C.   **Max.Size**: 15 cm.
Water: pH 6-7.5.   **Aquarium**: 120 cm.
Difficulty: 2.
Comments: Omnivorous. Eats all normal foods. Peaceful. Shy. Lively shoaling fish. Sensitive to bad water quality. Lot of open swimming place. Jumps.

Killifishes — Egg-Laying Toothcarps

The killifishes are famous for the way they have adapted to ensure species survival despite living in pools of water that dry up completely during the dry season in their natural habitat. Before the pool dries up they spawn, depositing their eggs in the upper layers of the substrate. The adult fishes then die, but when the next rainy season comes, and the pool is once again filled with water, the eggs hatch and the brief life cycle begins anew. Because of their short life-span they grow fast, in order to reach mature size within the few months before next dry season. In the aquarium they usually live longer than just a few months.

However, not all killifishes are "annual, fishes", and there are also a lot of "killis" with a more normal life cycle. These fishes live, in nature, in pools and streams that do not dry up during the dry season. Killifishes are found in most of Africa, southern Asia, North, Central, and South America, and Europe. With a few exceptions killis are small fishes (max. 10 cm). Many species prefer softly, slightly acid water There are, howovor, exceptions — so read the information for each species.

The males are often extremely colourful, while the females are rather more subdued in their coloration. As is often the case with very colourful fishes, the males can be aggressive towards conspecific males and those of similar species, so it may be better to have only one male (unless the aquarium is big — more than 150 l) along with several females. Sometimes is it possible to mix killis with other kinds of fishes that are about the same size and have similar requirements. You must take into consideration the fact that killis are relatively timid and there is a significant that they may go short of food in a mixed aquarium, so a special aquarium is better. An aquarium for killifishes should contain plenty of cover.

Most killis are carnivorous, feeding in nature on insects, larvae, and fish fry, and they have a somewhat more specialised food requirement than many other fishes; they specifically do not appreciate a diet of flake food alone. They prefer live foods such as newly-hatched brine shrimp or glass-worms (transparent mosquito larvae), but frozen foods are also accepted, e.g. glassworm and *Cyclops*.

Charley grimes

Mark Smith

Name: *Aphyosemion australe*
Family: Aplocheilidae.
Trade name: Lyretail panchax.
Range: Gabon, Angola, Cameroon.
Temp: 22-25°C.   **Max.Size:** 6 cm.
Water: pH 5.5-7.0. **Aquarium:** 50 cm.
Difficulty: 3.
Comments: Carnivorous. Needs live foods, but may accept frozen/dry foods. Substrate spawner. Dense planting. Very peaceful, but males are aggressive towards its own kind. A golden form exists. Jumps.

Name: *Aphyosemion gardneri gardneri*
Family: Aplocheilidae.
Trade name: Blue lyretail.
Range: Nigeria.
Temp: 22-26°C.   **Max.Size:** 6.5 cm.
Water: pH 5.5-7.0. **Aquarium:** 60 cm.
Difficulty: 3.
Comments: Carnivorous. Needs live foods, but may accept frozen/dry foods. Substrate (bottom) spawner. Dense planting. Peaceful. Several colour strains are available. Jumps.

Mark Smith

Mark Smith

Name: *Aphyosemion sjoestedti*
Family: Aplocheilidae.
Trade name: Blue gularis, golden pheasant.
Range: West Africa.
Temp: 22-26°C.   **Max.Size:** 14 cm.
Water: pH 6.0-7.0. **Aquarium:** 80 cm.
Difficulty: 3.
Comments: Carnivorous. Needs live foods, but may accept frozen/dry foods. Substrate (bottom) spawner. Rather aggressive. Dense planting. Annual. Jumps.

Name: *Aplocheilichthys pumilus*
Family: Poeciliidae.
Trade name: Tanganyika lampeye.
Range: East Africa lakes.
Temp: 24-26°C.   **Max.Size:** 5,5 cm.
Water: pH 7.0-7.5. **Aquarium:** 60 cm.
Difficulty: 3.
Comments: Omnivorous and carnivorous. Needs live foods, but may accept frozen/dry foods. Dense planting. Shoaling fish. Substrate (adhesive) spawner. Shy. Peaceful. Jumps.

Mark Smith

Mark Smith

Name: *Epiplatys annulatus*
Family: Aplocheilidae.
Trade name: Clown killie, Chocolate killie.
Range: Africa: from Guinea to Niger.
Temp: 23-26°C.   **Max.Size:** 4 cm.
Water: pH 6.0-7.0. **Aquarium:** 60 cm.
Difficulty: 4.
Comments: Carnivorous. Needs live foods, but may eat frozen/dry foods. Some plants in the aquarium. Adhesive spawner. Peaceful. Jumps. Delicate.

Name: *Epiplatys sexfasciatus*
Family: Aplocheilidae.
Trade name: Sixbanded panchax.
Range: West Africa.
Temp: 22-26°C.   **Max.Size:** 10 cm.
Water: pH 6.0-6.5. **Aquarium:** 100 cm.
Difficulty: 3.
Comments: Omnivorous. Needs live foods, but may accept frozen/dry foods. Aggressive. Adhesive spawner. Needs hiding-places. Jumps.

Mark Smith

Mark Smith

Name: *Jordanella floridae*
Family: Cyprinodontidae.
Trade name: American flagfish, Florida flagfioh.
Range: South-eastern North America.
Temp: 18-22°C.   **Max.Size:** 6.5 cm.
Water: pH 6.5-7.5. **Aquarium:** 60 cm.
Difficulty: 2.
Comments: Omnivorous. Eats all normal foods. Very aggressive. Dense planting. Substrate brooder. Jumps.

Name: *Lamprichthys tanganicanus*
Family: Poeciliidae.
Trade name: Tanganyika killi.
Range: Africa: Lake Tanganyika.
Temp: 24-26°C.   **Max.Size:** 16 cm.
Water: pH 8.0-8.5. **Aquarium:** 100 cm.
Difficulty: 4.
Comments: Carnivorous. Needs live foods, but may eat frozen/dry foods. Shoaling fish. Continuous substrate egg scatterer. Shy. Territorial. Sensitive to transport. Needs caves in the aquarium with flat stones. Jumps.

Name: *Nothobranchius kirkii*
Family: Aplocheilidae.
Trade name: Kirk's notho.
Range: East Africa, Malawi.
Temp: 22-26°C. **Max.Size:** 5 cm.
Water: pH 6.5-7.5. **Aquarium:** 50 cm.
Difficulty: 4.
Comments: Carnivorous. Needs live foods, but may eat frozen/dry foods. Substrate (bottom) spawner. Territorial and aggressive towards its own kind. Annual fish. Needs hiding-places. Jumps.

Name: *Nothobranchius guentheri*
Family: Aplocheilidae.
Trade name: Redtail notho, Günther's notho.
Range: Africa. Zanzibar.
Temp: 22-25°C. **Max.Size:** 6,5 cm.
Water: pH 6.0-7.0. **Aquarium:** 50 cm.
Difficulty: 4.
Comments: Carnivorous. Needs live foods but may eat frozen/dry foods. Substrate (bottom) spawner. Territorial and aggressive towards its own kind. Annual fish. Needs hiding-places. Jumps.

Name: *Nothobranchius palmqvisti*
Family: Aplocheilidae.
Trade name: Palmqvist's notho.
Range: Kenya, Tanzania.
Temp: 18-22°C. **Max.Size:** 5 cm.
Water: pH 6.5-7.0. **Aquarium:** 50 cm.
Difficulty: 4.
Comments: Carnivorous. Needs live foods, but may eat frozen/dry foods. Continuous substrate (bottom) spawner. Territorial and aggressive. Dense planting. Jumps.

Name: *Oxyzygonectes dovii*
Family: Anablepidae.
Trade name: *Aplocheilus dovii.*
Range: Pacific Coast.
Temp: 22-28°C. **Max.Size:** 35 cm.
Water: pH 6.0-7.5. **Aquarium:** 200 cm.
Difficulty: 4.
Comments: Carnivorous. Needs live foods, but may eat frozen/dry foods. Substrate spawner. Peaceful. Shy. Needs hiding-places. Jumps.

Labyrinth Fishes (anabantoids)

The labyrinth fishes' natural habitat is the major part of Africa but above all southeast Asia. It is in Asia that we find those fishes that are most common in our aquaria. The best known of these are the gouramis and the fighting fishes of the genus *Betta*.

The name labyrinth fish refers to the special accessory respiratory organ (the labyrinth) these fishes possess as an adaptation to life in the oxygen-poor water of their natural habitat (rice fields, ditches etc.). This respiratory organ allows the fishes to breathe atmospheric air as well as taking oxygen from the water via their gills as in other fishes. Because of this air-breathing it is important that the air above the water's surface is humid and has the same temperature as the water in the aquarium. If for any reason these fishes are unable to reach the water's surface they will "drown", regardless of the oxygen content of the aquarium water.

Most labyrinth fishes are very suitable as aquarium fishes since they are small and beautiful, even if there are some exceptions like the giant gourami (*Osphronemus gorami*), which can grow up to 75 cm long.

These fishes have a relatively wide tolerance as regards water parameters, but fairly neutral water is preferable for most species. Even though they are relatively hardy fishes they prefer a peaceful environment with shady cover. The filter current mustn't be too strong. The genus *Colisa* (dwarf gouramis) is rather more delicate (see Especially sensitive species). For additional information about decor, etc. read the first general section of this book.

Many species within this group are bubble-nest builders (see BREEDING). The bubble nest varies from small to large, stable to fragile, and free-floating to anchored among plants or even inside a cave (cave spawners). Not all labyrinth fishes are bubble-nest builders; some are mouthbrooders and cave spawners as mentioned. In general the males have more intense colours than the females.

Name: *Anabas testudineus*
Family: Anabantidae.
Trade name: Climbing perch.
Habitat: Tropical Asia.
Temp: 22-30°C.   **Max.Size**: 25 cm.
Water: pH 6.5-7.5. **Aquarium**: 120 cm.
Difficulty: 3
Comments: Omnivorous. Eats all normal foods. Aggressive. Keep only with large fishes. Shy. Floating eggs. Jumps. Can "walk" on land. Needs floating plants and hiding-places. Tolerates brackish water.

Name: *Belontia signata*
Family: Belontiidae.
Trade name: Comb-tailed paradise fish, Combtail.
Habitat: Southwest Asia.
Temp: 24-28°C.   **Max.Size**: 18 cm.
Water: pH 6.5-7.5. **Aquarium**: 100 cm.
Difficulty: 3
Comments: Omnivorous. Eats all normal foods. Eggs attached to underside of plant leaves. Young specimens are peaceful. Adults are aggressive. Keep only with large fishes. Needs densely planted aquarium and hiding-places.

Name: *Betta imbellis*
Family: Belontiidae.
Trade name: Peaceful betta, Crescent.
Habitat: Malayan peninsula, Indonesia.
Temp: 25-28°C.   **Max.Size**: 5.5 cm.
Water: pH 5.5-7. **Aquarium**: 100 cm.
Difficulty: 3
Comments: Carnivorous. Eats all normal foods. Bubblenest. Territorial but relatively peaceful, compared with *Betta splendens*. One male (+females) in a 40 cm aquarium. Two males in a 100 cm aquarium. Floating plants.

Name: *Colisa chuna*
Family: Belontiidae.
Trade name: *Colisa sota*, Honey gourami.
Habitat: India, Bangladesh.
Temp: 23-28°C.   **Max.Size**: 7 cm.
Water: pH 6-7.5. **Aquarium**: 50 cm.
Difficulty: 3
Comments: Omnivorous. Eats all normal foods, but some live foods necessary. Loose bubblenest. Peaceful. Shy. Territorial when breeding. Sensitive to velvet disease. Densely planted aquarium with floating plants.

Betta splendens

Betta splendens

Betta splendens

Betta splendens

Betta splendens

Name: *Betta splendens*
Family: Belontiidae.
Trade name: Siamese fighting fish.
Habitat: Thailand, Cambodia.
Temp: 25-30°C.   **Max.Size**: 5 cm.
Water: pH 6-8.   **Aquarium**: 40 cm.
Difficulty: 3
Comments: Carnivorous. Eats all normal foods. Bubblenest. Extremely aggressive — males cannot be kept together. Some plants are necessary.

Name: *Colisa fasciata*
Family: Belontiidae.
Trade name: Banded gourami.
Habitat: Tropical Asia.
Temp: 23-28°C.   **Max.Size**: 12 cm.
Water: pH 6-7.5.   **Aquarium**: 70 cm.
Difficulty: 3
Comments: Omnivorous. Eats all normal foods. Bubblenest. Peaceful. Territorial when breeding. Some plants, but also an open swimming area. Sensitive to bad water quality.

Name: *Colisa labiosa*
Family: Belontiidae.
Trade name: Thick-lipped gourami.
Habitat: Asia: Southern Myanmar.
Temp: 23-28°C. **Max.Size**: 9 cm.
Water: pH 6-7.5. **Aquarium**: 60 cm.
Difficulty: 2
Comments: Omnivorous. Eats all normal foods. Bubblenest, but doesn't use plants in the construction. Peaceful. Sensitive to bad water quality. Relatively dense planting.

Name: *Colisa lalia*
Family: Belontiidae.
Trade name: Dwarf gourami.
Habitat: India, Pakistan, Bangladesh.
Temp: 25-28°C. **Max.Size**: 8 cm.
Water: pH 6-7.5. **Aquarium**: 60 cm.
Difficulty: 2
Comments: Omnivorous. Eats all normal foods. Bubblenest. Peaceful. Shy. Sensitive to bad water quality. Relatively dense planting and floating plants. Popular aquarium fish. Sometimes bad quality, probably because of inbreeding.

Name: *Ctenopoma acutirostre*
Family: Anabantidae.
Trade name: Leopard bushfish, spotted Ctenopoma.
Habitat: Zaire.
Temp: 20-26°C. **Max.Size**: 15 cm.
Water: pH 6-7.5. **Aquarium**: 90 cm.
Difficulty: 4
Comments: Carnivorous. Live food. Bubblenest. Peaceful.

Name: *Helostoma temminckii*
Family: Helostomidae.
Trade name: Kissing gourami.
Habitat: Thailand, Malay Peninsula, Indonesia.
Temp: 23-28°C. **Max.Size**: 35 cm.
Water: pH 6-8. **Aquarium**: 200 cm.
Difficulty: 4.
Comments: Omnivorous and herbivorous. Eats plants. Eats all normal foods. Floating eggs. Males fight with each other. Too big for many domestic aquaria.

Name: *Macropodus opercularis*
Family: Belontiidae.
Trade name: Paradise fish.
Habitat: Southeast Asia.
Temp: 18-25°C.　　**Max.Size**: 10 cm.
Water: pH 6-8.　　**Aquarium**: 80 cm.
Difficulty: 2.
Comments: Omnivorous. Eats all normal foods. Bubblenest. Males are extremely aggressive towards males of its own kind. Probably the second (after goldfish) ornamental fish to be introduced into Europe.

Name: *Parosphromenus deissneri*
Family: Belontiidae.
Trade name: Licorice gourami.
Habitat: Malaysia, Singapore, Indonesia.
Temp: 25-28°C.　　**Max.Size**: 4 cm.
Water: pH 6-7.　　**Aquarium**: 60 cm.
Difficulty: 4.
Comments: Carnivorous. Eats all normal foods, but prefers live foods. Substrate (cave) brooder. Peaceful. Very sensitive. Dense planting.

Name: *Sphaerichthys osphromenoides.*
Family: Belontiidae.
Trade name: Chocolate gourami.
Habitat: Indonesia, Malay Peninsula.
Temp: 25-27°C.　　**Max.Size**: 6 cm.
Water: pH 4-6.5.　　**Aquarium**: 70 cm.
Difficulty: 4.
Comments: Omnivorous. Eats all normal foods, but live foods necessary. Mouthbrooder. Peaceful. Shy. Very sensitive. Dense planting.

Name: *Trichogaster leeri*
Family: Belontiidae.
Trade name: Pearl gourami.
Habitat: Indonesia, Malay Peninsula, Thailand.
Temp: 24-28°C.　　**Max.Size**: 12 cm.
Water: pH 6-7.5.　　**Aquarium**: 70 cm.
Difficulty: 1.
Comments: Omnivorous and carnivorous. Eats all normal foods. Bubblenest. Peaceful, but males may fight with each other. Popular aquarium fish and one of the most hardy of all labyrinths.

Name: *Trichogaster microlepis*
Family: Belontiidae.
Trade name: Moonlight gourami.
Habitat: Thailand.
Temp: 25-30°C. **Max.Size**: 15 cm.
Water: pH 6-7. **Aquarium**: 100 cm.
Difficulty: 3.
Comments: Omnivorous and carnivorous. Eats all normal foods. Bubblenest. Peaceful, but males may fight with each other. Dense planting but not with fine-leaved plants.

Name: *Trichogaster pectoralis*
Family: Belontiidae.
Trade name: Snakeskin gourami.
Habitat: Thailand, Malaysia, Cambodia, Vietnam.
Temp: 23-28°C. **Max.Size**: 25 cm.
Water: pH 6-8. **Aquarium**: 100 cm.
Difficulty: 1.
Comments: Omnivorous. Eats all normal foods. Bubblenest. Very peaceful. Dense planting.

Name: *Trichogaster trichopterus*
Family: Belontiidae.
Trade name: Blue-, spotted-, or gold gourami.
Habitat: Laos, Cambodia, Vietnam, Thailand. **Temp**: 22-28°C.
Max.Size: 15 cm. **Water**: pH 6-7.5.
Aquarium: 80 cm. **Difficulty**: 1.
Comments: Omnivorous. Eats all normal foods. Bubblenest. Very peaceful, but males may fight with each other. Several colour morphs exist. Dense planting. Popular aquarium fish.

Name: *Trichopsis pumila*
Family: Belontiidae.
Trade name: Dwarf croaking gourami, pygmy gourami.
Habitat: Vietnam, Thailand, Malaysia.
Temp: 25-28°C. **Max.Size**: 3,5 cm.
Water: pH 6-7. **Aquarium**: 60 cm.
Difficulty: 4.
Comments: Omnivorous and carnivorous. Eats all small normal foods. Bubblenest. Peaceful, but somewhat aggressive when breeding. Dense planting.

Rainbowfishes

During the past few years the rainbowfishes have become very popular among hobbyists. They would probably have been even more popular if the juveniles had the same splendid colours as the adults. The colours of males in particular are "something else". Unfortunately it is commonly juveniles that are found in aquarium shops, and hence the customer may remain unaware of the splendid adult colours.

The habitat of most rainbowfishes is in the Australasian region, but they are also found in other localities (e.g. Madagascar). In nature they live in clear, oxygen-rich water and therefore a relatively powerful filtration is required in the aquarium. The water should be neutral with a pH of 7 or slightly higher. It is not only the colours that have made them popular, but also that many are relatively easy to keep in the aquarium. Most are shoaling fishes and hence it is better to buy a number of each species (6-10). In addition males exhibit better coloration if there are several males competing for the females. They prefer plenty of plants in the aquarium and some rocks and wood can also readily be incorporated into the decor. Plants are necessary since most species when they are breeding scatter the eggs among the plants. Rainbow fishes are not problematical regarding food. They will normally eat what they are offered. Flake food and granulated food are taken readily, and if they every now and then receive frozen food e.g. glassworm, mosquito larvae, and *Cyclops*, then they don't say no. It is possible to mix them with other kinds of fishes of about the same size, without any major problems. There are, however, many different kinds of rainbowfishes in the trade so there is really no need to mix them with other fishes at all.

Name: *Bedotia geayi*
Family: Bedotiidae
Trade name: Madagascar rainbow.
Habitat: Madagascar.
Temp: 20-25°C.   **Max.Size:** 12 cm.
Water: pH 7.0-8.0. **Aquarium:** 100 cm.
Difficulty: 3
Comments: Omnivorous and carnivorous. Eats all normal foods. Eggs scattered among plants. Shoaling fish. Lively fish. Peaceful. Jumps. Aquarium with plants and a large swimming area.

Name: *Glossolepis incisus*
Family: Melanotaeniidae.
Trade name: Red rainbowfish.
Habitat: Papua New Guinea: Lake Sentani; Indonesia..
Temp: 22-24°C.   **Max.Size:** 15 cm.
Water: pH 7.0-8.0. **Aquarium:** 100 cm.
Difficulty: 3
Comments: Omnivorous and carnivorous. Needs frozen or live foods. Eggs scattered among plants. Shoaling fish. Lively fish. Peaceful. Jumps. Aquarium with plants and a large swimming area.

Name: *Marosatherina ladigesi*
Family: Telmatherinidae.
Trade name: Celebes rainbowfish, *Telmatherina ladigesi.*
Habitat: Indonesia: southern Sulawesi.
Temp: 22-28°C.   **Max.Size:** 9 cm.
Water: pH 6.5-8.0. **Aquarium:** 80 cm.
Difficulty: 3   **Comments:** Omnivorous. Needs frozen or live foods. Eggs scattered among plants. Shoaling fish. Lively fish. Peaceful. Sensitive to transportation. Aquarium with plants and a large swimming area. Jumps.

Name: *Melanotaenia affinis*
Family: Melanotaeniidae.
Trade name: North New Guinea rainbowfish.
Habitat: Papua New Guinea.
Temp: 20-30°C.   **Max.Size:** 12 cm.
Water: pH 7.0-8.0. **Aquarium:** 80 cm.
Difficulty: 3
Comments: Omnivorous. Needs frozen or live foods. Eggs scattered among plants. Shoaling fish. Lively fish. Peaceful. Jumps. Aquarium with plants and a large swimming area.

Name: *Melanotaenia boesemani*
Family: Melanotaeniidae.
Trade name: Boeseman's rainbow.
Habitat: Papua New Guinea, Indonesia.
Temp: 26-30°C.   **Max.Size:** 11 cm.
Water: pH 7.0-8.0. **Aquarium:** 100 cm.
Difficulty: 3
Comments: Omnivorous. Needs frozen or live foods. Eggs scattered continuously among plants. Shoaling fish. Lively fish. Peaceful. Jumps. Aquarium with plants and a large swimming area.

Name: *Melanotaenia kamaka*
Family: Melanotaeniidae.
Trade name: Kamaka rainbowfish.
Habitat: Papua New Guinea. Lake Kamaka; Indonesia.
Temp: 25-29°C.   Max.Size: 8 cm.
Water: pH 7.0-8.0. Aquarium: 80 cm.
Difficulty: 3
Comments: Omnivorous and carnivorous. Needs frozen or live foods. Eggs scattered among plants. Shoaling fish. Lively fish. Peaceful. Jumps. Aquarium with plants and a large swimming area.

Name: *Melanotaenia lacustris*
Family: Melanotaeniidae.
Trade name: Lake Kutubu rainbowfish.
Habitat: Papua New Guinea. Lake Kutubu.
Temp: 20-25°C.   Max.Size: 12 cm.
Water: pH 7.0-8.0. Aquarium: 100 cm.
Difficulty: 3
Comments: Omnivorous. Eats all normal foods. Eggs scattered among plants. Shoaling fish. Lively fish. Peaceful. Jumps. Aquarium with plants and a large swimming area.

Name: M*elanotaenia maccullochi*
Family: Melanotaeniidae.
Trade name: Black-line rainbowfish.
Habitat: Northeast Australia, Papua New Guinea.
Temp: 20-26°C.   Max.Size: 7 cm.
Water: pH 7.0-8.0. Aquarium: 80 cm.
Difficulty: 3
Comments: Omnivorous. Need frozen or live foods. Eggs scattered among plants. Shoaling fish. Lively fish. Peaceful. Jumps. Aquarium with plants and a large swimming area.

Name: *Melanotaenia parkinsoni*
Family: Melanotaeniidae.
Trade name: Parkinson's rainbowfish.
Habitat: Papua New Guinea: Kamp Welsh River.
Temp: 24-28°C.   Max.Size: 13 cm.
Water: pH 7.0-8.0. Aquarium: 100 cm.
Difficulty: 3
Comments: Omnivorous and carnivorous. Needs frozen or live foods. Eggs scattered among plants. Shoaling fish. Lively fish. Peaceful. Jumps. Aquarium with plants and a large swimming area.

Name: *Melanotaenia praecox*
Family: Melanotaeniidae.
Trade name: Neon rainbowfish.
Habitat: Papua New Guinea: Irian Jaya; Indonesia.
Temp: 22-28°C.   **Max.Size:** 6 cm.
Water: pH 7.0-8.0. **Aquarium:** 80 cm.
Difficulty: 3
Comments: Omnivorous. Needs frozen or live foods. Eggs scattered among plants. Shoaling fish. Lively fish. Peaceful. Jumps. Aquarium with plants and a large swimming area.

Name: *Melanotaenia pygmaea*
Family: Melanotaeniidae.
Trade name: Pygmy rainbowfish.
Habitat: Australia: Prince Regent river area.
Temp: 22-26°C.   **Max.Size:** 7 cm.
Water: pH 7.0-8.0. **Aquarium:** 80 cm.
Difficulty: 4
Comments: Omnivorous. Needs frozen or live foods. Eggs scattered among plants. Shoaling fish. Peaceful. Lively fish. Jumps. Aquarium with plants and a large swimming area.

Name: *Melanotaenia trifasciata*
Family: Melanotaeniidae.
Trade name: Banded rainbowfish.
Habitat: Australia.
Temp: 24-30°C.   **Max.Size:** 12 cm.
Water: pH 7.0-8.0. **Aquarium:** 100 cm.
Difficulty: 3
Comments: Omnivorous and carnivorous. Needs frozen or live foods. Eggs scattered among plants. Shoaling fish. Lively fish. Peaceful. Exists in several colour variants. Jumps. Aquarium with plants and a large swimming area.

Name: *Pseudomugil furcatus*
Family: Pseudomugilidae.
Trade name: Forktail rainbowfish.
Habitat: Eastern Papua New Guinea.
Temp: 24-26°C.   **Max.Size:** 6 cm.
Water: pH 6.5-8.0. **Aquarium:** 60 cm.
Difficulty: 3
Comments: Omnivorous and carnivorous. Needs frozen or live foods. Eggs scattered among plants. Shoaling fish. Lively fish. Peaceful. Jumps. Aquarium with plants and a large swimming area.

Catfishes

Most aquaria contain one or more catfishes, even though often the reason for their inclusion is that they are regarded as the garbage-collectors of the aquarium, something that is correct, at least in part. There are numerous species of catfishes (Siluriformes) found all over the world, but they are most common in South America and Africa. It is a fact that there are more than 2000 different scientifically described species. They range from tiny catfishes such as the pygmy cory (*Corydoras pygmaeus*) to huge species such as the red-tailed catfish (*Phractocephalus hemioliopterus*) which is a predator more than one metre long. The latter species is hardly suitable for the aquarium.

The skin of catfishes is either "naked" or protected by bony plates called scutes. All species have barbels, sensory appendages ("feelers") located around the mouth, and in some species these are often very long and slender like the whiskers of a cat — hence the name "catfish". These barbels are covered in taste-buds which enable the catfish to detect food, either by contact or by "smelling" it in the water, and they can also detect other fishes by the same means.

The catfishes are subdivided into a number of groups. The species most commonly kept as aquarium fishes are the mailed catfishes (e.g. *Corydoras*) and the armoured catfishes (*Loricariidae*) — the latter are also commonly known as suckermouth catfishes. Both these groups come from South America. Also fairly commonplace are the *Synodontis* species (upside-down catfishes) from Africa.

Catfishes are very often kept together with other fishes in the aquarium, which is fine as they also live together with other fishes in nature. It is important to remember that many catfishes are active at nights (nocturnal), which means that the aquarium must contain hiding-places to which they can retire during the day. Hiding-places can be made using wood and rocks, and plants can also provide shelter.

It is also important to remember that they are nocturnal when feeding the fishes, and to put some catfish tablets (that sink) in the aquarium (always in the same place) immediately after the in the aquarium light is switched off for the night. Moreover, while it is true that many catfishes are good scavengers (garbage-collectors) in the aquarium, it is wrong to assume that they can live just on leftover food and algae. There are very good catfish tablets available in the trade that are formulated for both the algae-eating species and those that scavenge on the bottom (e.g. *Corydoras*).

It has been mentioned earlier, in the first section of this book (see PLANTS), that several catfish species (especially the Loricariid group) feed on algae in the aquarium and should therefore be introduced right from the start. Many other species scavenge on the substrate and in this way help keep the bottom clean. They are not only useful fishes but also very interesting, and this is an additional reason to have them in the aquarium. They also liven up the bottom of the aquarium, an area that many other types of fishes rarely if ever frequent.

Catfishes are usually relatively adaptable as regards water conditions and will tolerate a wide spectrum of pH, hardness, and temperature. Most species prefer relatively neutral water (pH 6.5-7.4) with a temperature of 23-26° C, but the species from lakes Malawi and Tanganyika prefer more alkaline water.

Name: *Agamyxis pectinifrons*
Family: Doradidae
Trade name: White-spotted talking catfish.
Range: South America
Temp: 22-26°C   **Max.Size**: 16 cm.
Water: pH 6-7.5.   **Aquarium**: 100 cm.
Difficulty: 2.
Comments: Omnivorous. Nocturnal. Substrate (among floating plants) spawner. May eat very small fishes. Needs several hiding-places (rocks or wood).

Name: *Ancistrus ranunculus*
Family: Loricariidae.
Trade name: Frog bristlenose. L 34.
Range: Brazil: Xingu, Rio Tocantins.
Temp: 24-27°C   **Max.Size**: 15 cm.
Water: pH 6-7.5.   **Aquarium**: 100 cm.
Difficulty: 3.
Comments: Herbivorous and omnivorous. Algae-eater. Substrate (cave) brooder. Mostly nocturnal. Peaceful but territorial towards males of its own kind. Needs several hiding-places.

Name: *Ancistrus dolichopterus*
Family: Loricariidae.
Trade name: Bushymouth catfish, Bristlenose.
Range: Amazon basin.
Temp: 24-27°C   **Max.Size**: 13 cm.
Water: pH 6-8.   **Aquarium**: 80 cm.
Difficulty: 1.
Comments: Herbivorous. Algae-eater. Substrate (cave) brooder. Mostly nocturnal. Peaceful, but sometimes somewhat aggressive when breeding. Needs hiding-places. Common aquarium fish.

Name: *Arius seemanni*
Family: Ariidae.
Trade name: Shark catfish.
Range: Mexico to Peru.
Temp: 20-26°C   **Max.Size**: 35 cm.
Water: pH 7-8.   **Aquarium**: 200 cm.
Difficulty: 3.
Comments: Omnivorous and somewhat carnivorous. Prefers frozen and live foods. Mouthbrooder. Peaceful together with other large fishes. Territorial towards its own kind. Adult specimens prefer brackish water.

Name: *Auchenoglanis occidentalis*
Family: Bagridae.
Trade name: Giraffe-nosed catfish.
Range: Africa: tropics.
Temp: 20-26°C   **Max.Size**: 75 cm.
Water: pH 6.5-8.   **Aquarium**: 300 cm.
Difficulty: 5.
Comments: Omnivorous and piscivorous. Eats small fishes. Good food fish. Too big for normal aquaria.

Name: *Baryancistrus* sp. L85
Family: Loricariidae.
Trade name: Xingu Baryancistrus. L85.
Range: Brazil: Rio Xingú.
Temp: 22-25°C   **Max.Size**: 25 cm.
Water: pH 6.5-7.   **Aquarium**: 120 cm.
Difficulty: 3.
Comments: Omnivorous. Eats some algae. Substrate (cave) brooder. Mostly nocturnal.

Name: *Brochis britskii*
Family: Callichthyidae.
Trade name: Giant Brochis.
Range: Brazil: Rio Paraguay.
Temp: 22-25°C   **Max.Size**: 10 cm.
Water: pH 6.5-7.5. **Aquarium**: 80 cm.
Difficulty: 3.
Comments: Carnivorous. Needs frozen food, but also eats dry food. Substrate (among plants) spawner. Peaceful. Day-active. Needs fine sand (max 2 mm) without sharp edges.

Name: *Brochis splendens*
Family: Callichthyidae.
Trade name: Emerald Brochis.
Range: Brazil, Ecuador, Peru.
Temp: 22-27°C   **Max.Size**: 9 cm.
Water: pH 6.5-7.5. **Aquarium**: 80 cm.
Difficulty: 2.
Comments: Omnivorous and carnivorous. Frozen food, but also eats dry food. Substrate (among plants) spawner. Peaceful. Shoaling fish. Day-active. Needs fine sand (max 2 mm) without sharp edges.

Name: *Callichthys callichthys*
Family: Callichthyidae.
Trade name: Slender armoured catfish.
Range: Brazil, Bolivia, Peru, Venezuela, Paraguay.
Temp: 20-28°C   **Max.Size**: 13 cm.
Water: pH 6-8.   **Aquarium**: 100 cm.
Difficulty: 1.
Comments: Omnivorous and carnivorous. Adult specimens may eat very small fishes. Eats all normal foods. Bubblenest-brooder. Peaceful. Partly nocturnal. Needs several hiding-places.

Name: *Chaca chaca*
Family: Chacidae.
Trade name: Frogmouth or Squarehead catfish.
Range: India, Bangladesh, Nepal.
Temp: 22-25°C   **Max.Size**: 20 cm.
Water: pH 6-8.   **Aquarium**: 100 cm.
Difficulty: 4.
Comments: Carnivorous. Piscivorous — therefore to be hold only together with large fishes. Can be trained to accept pellets. Extremely nocturnal. Needs several hiding-places.

Mark Smith

Mark Smith

Name: *Corydoras adolfoi*
Family: Callichthyidae.
Trade name: Adolfo's cory.
Range: Brazil: Upper Rio Negro, Rio Uaupés.
Temp: 23-26°C   **Max.Size**: 5 cm.
Water: pH 6-7.5.   **Aquarium**: 60 cm.
Difficulty: 3.
Comments: Omnivorous and carnivorous. Shoaling fish. Peaceful. Attaches eggs to plants. All *Corydoras* need fine sand (max 2 mm) without sharp edges. Needs oxygen-rich water. Day-active.

Name: *Corydoras aeneus*
Family: Callichthyidae.
Trade name: Bronze corydoras.
Range: Venezuela to Brazil.
Temp: 24-27°C   **Max.Size**: 8.5 cm.
Water: pH 6-7.5.   **Aquarium**: 60 cm.
Difficulty: 2.
Comments: Omnivorous and carnivorous. Shoaling fish. Peaceful. Attaches eggs to plants All *Corydoras* need fine sand without sharp edges. A cultivated albino-form is also available. Day-active.

Mark Smith

Mark Smith

Name: *Corydoras araguaiaensis*
Family: Callichthyidae.
Trade name: Araguaia cory.
Range: Brazil: Rio Araguaia.
Temp: 23-26°C   **Max.Size**: 5.5 cm.
Water: pH 6-7.5.   **Aquarium**: 60 cm.
Difficulty: 3.
Comments: Omnivorous. Shoaling fish. Peaceful. Attaches eggs to plants. All *Corydoras* need fine sand (max 2 mm) without sharp edges. Needs oxygen-rich water. Day-active.

Name: *Corydoras barbatus*
Family: Callichthyidae.
Trade name: Bearded corydoras.
Range: Southern Brazil.
Temp: 24-27°C   **Max.Size**: 12 cm.
Water: pH 6-7.5.   **Aquarium**: 100 cm.
Difficulty: 2.
Comments: Omnivorous and carnivorous. Shoaling fish. Peaceful. Attaches eggs to plants. All *Corydoras* need fine sand (max 2 mm) without sharp edges. Day-active.

Name: *Corydoras elegans*
Family: Callichthyidae.
Trade name: Elegant cory.
Range: Brazil: Amazon region.
Temp: 23-26°C   **Max.Size**: 6 cm.
Water: pH 6-7.5.   **Aquarium**: 60 cm.
Difficulty: 2.
Comments: Omnivorous and carnivorous. Shoaling fish. Peaceful. Attaches eggs to plants. All *Corydoras* need fine sand (max 2 mm) without sharp edges. Day-active.

Name: *Corydoras habrosus*
Family: Callichthyidae.
Trade name: Salt and pepper cory.
Range: Colombia, Venezuela.
Temp: 24-27°C   **Max.Size**: 2.5 cm.
Water: pH 6-7.   **Aquarium**: 60 cm.
Difficulty: 3.
Comments: Omnivorous and carnivorous. Shoaling fish. Peaceful. Attaches eggs to plants. All *Corydoras* need fine sand (max 2 mm) without sharp edges. Day-active.

Name: *Corydoras julii*
Family: Callichthyidae.
Trade name: Leopard corydoras.
Range: Brazil: Amazon basin.
Temp: 23-26°C   **Max.Size**: 6 cm.
Water: pH 6-7.5.   **Aquarium**: 60 cm.
Difficulty: 4.
Comments: Omnivorous and carnivorous. Shoaling fish. Peaceful. Attaches eggs to plants. All *Corydoras* need fine sand (max 2 mm) without sharp edges. Day-active. Rather delicate.

Name: *Corydoras metae*
Family: Callichthyidae.
Trade name: Masked corydoras.
Range: Colombia: Rio Meta.
Temp: 23-26°C   **Max.Size**: 5,5 cm.
Water: pH 6-7.5.   **Aquarium**: 60 cm.
Difficulty: 2.
Comments: Omnivorous and carnivorous. Shoaling fish. Peaceful. Attaches eggs to plants. All *Corydoras* need fine sand (max 2 mm) without sharp edges. Day-active.

Name: *Corydoras paleatus*
Family: Callichthyidae.
Trade name: Peppered corydoras.
Range: Southern Brazil to Argentina.
Temp: 20-25°C   **Max.Size**: 8 cm.
Water: pH 6.5-7.5. **Aquarium**: 70 cm.
Difficulty: 2.
Comments: Omnivorous and carnivorous. Shoaling fish. Peaceful. Attaches eggs to plants. All *Corydoras* need fine sand (max 2 mm) without sharp edges. Farmed in huge quantities. Day-active.

Name: *Corydoras panda*
Family: Callichthyidae.
Trade name: Panda Corydoras.
Range: Peru: Ucayali Basin.
Temp: 22-25°C   **Max.Size**: 4.5 cm.
Water: pH 6.5-7.5. **Aquarium**: 60 cm.
Difficulty: 3.
Comments: Omnivorous and carnivorous. Shoaling fish. Peaceful. Attaches eggs to plants. All *Corydoras* need fine sand (max 2 mm) without sharp edges. Day-active.

Name: *Corydoras pygmaeus*
Family: Callichthyidae.
Trade name: Pygmy Corydoras.
Range: Brazil: Rio Madeira.
Temp: 23-26°C   **Max.Size**: 2,5 cm.
Water: pH 6-7.   **Aquarium**: 60 cm.
Difficulty: 4.
Comments: Omnivorous and carnivorous. Shoaling fish. Peaceful. Attaches eggs to plants. All *Corydoras* need fine sand (max 2 mm) without sharp edges. Day-active. Rather delicate.

Name: *Corydoras rabauti*
Family: Callichthyidae.
Trade name: Rusty Corydoras.
Range: Amazon basin.
Temp: 23-26°C   **Max.Size**: 6 cm.
Water: pH 6-7.5.   **Aquarium**: 60 cm.
Difficulty: 3.
Comments: Omnivorous and carnivorous. Shoaling fish. Peaceful. Attaches eggs to plants. All *Corydoras* need fine sand (max 2 mm) without sharp edges. Day-active.

Name: *Corydoras reticulatus*
Family: Callichthyidae.
Trade name: Reticulated or network Corydoras.
Range: Amazon basin.
Temp: 23-26°C **Max.Size**: 7 cm.
Water: pH 6-7.5. **Aquarium**: 60 cm.
Difficulty: 3.
Comments: Omnivorous. Shoaling fish. Peaceful. Attaches eggs to plants. All *Corydoras* need fine sand (max 2 mm) without sharp edges. Needs oxygen-rich water. Day-active.

Name: *Corydoras robineae*
Family: Callichthyidae.
Trade name: Flagtail Corydoras.
Range: Brazil: upper Rio Negro.
Temp: 23-26°C **Max.Size**: 7 cm.
Water: pH 6-7. **Aquarium**: 70 cm.
Difficulty: 3.
Comments: Omnivorous and carnivorous. Shoaling fish. Peaceful. Attaches eggs to plants. All *Corydoras* need fine sand (max 2 mm) without sharp edges. Needs oxygen-rich water. Day-active.

Name: *Corydoras sterbai*
Family: Callichthyidae.
Trade name: Sterba's corydoras.
Range: Brazil: Rio Guaporé, Bolivia.
Temp: 22-25°C **Max.Size**: 8 cm.
Water: pH 6-7. **Aquarium**: 80 cm.
Difficulty: 2.
Comments: Omnivorous and carnivorous. Shoaling fish. Peaceful. Attaches eggs to plants. All *Corydoras* need fine sand (max 2 mm) without sharp edges. Needs oxygen-rich water.

Name: *Dysichthys coracoideus*
Family: Aspredinidae.
Trade name: Bicoloured banjo catfish.
Range: Amazon basin.
Temp: 23-26°C **Max.Size**: 15 cm.
Water: pH 6-8. **Aquarium**: 100 cm.
Difficulty: 3.
Comments: Carnivorous. Live and frozen food. Peaceful. Substrate brooder. Crepuscular and nocturnal. Needs fine sand (max 2 mm) without sharp edges.

Name: *Farlowella gracilis*
Family: Loricariidae.
Trade name: Mottled twig catfish.
Range: Colombia.
Temp: 24-26°C   **Max.Size**: 19 cm.
Water: pH 6-7.   **Aquarium**: 80 cm.
Difficulty: 4.
Comments: Herbivorous. Algae-eater. Substrate (plants) brooder. Pairing fish. Peaceful. Sensitive. Needs oxygen-rich water of high quality and a mature aquarium.

Name: *Glyptoperichthys gibbiceps*
Family: Loricariidae.
Trade name: *Pterygoplichthys gibbiceps*, Sailfin pleco, Leopard pleco.
Range: Amazonas and Orinoco basins.
Temp: 23-27°C   **Max.Size**: 50 cm.
Water: pH 6-8.   **Aquarium**: 160 cm.
Difficulty: 1.
Comments: Herbivorous and omnivorous. Algae-eater. Peaceful, but large males are territorial towards their own kind. Only for large aquaria.

Name: *Hara hara*
Family: Sisoridae.
Range: India, Nepal, Bangladesh.
Temp: 18-28°C   **Max.Size**: 7 cm.
Water: pH 6.5-7.5. **Aquarium**: 80 cm.
Difficulty: 3.
Comments: Omnivorous. Prefers live-food. Shoaling fish. Planted aquarium. Peaceful. Nocturnal. Needs oxygen-rich water of high quality.

Name: *Hemiancistrus* sp. L174
Family: Loricariidae.
Trade name: *Ancistrus* sp. L174. Black and white ancistrus.
Range: Brazil: Rio Xingú.
Temp: 23-27°C   **Max.Size**: 15 cm.
Water: pH 6-7.5.   **Aquarium**: 120 cm.
Difficulty: 3.
Comments: Herbivorous and omnivorous. Algae-eater. Substrate (cave) brooder. Peaceful. Nocturnal.

Name: *Hoplosternum littorale*
Family: Callichthyidae.
Trade name: Clay hoplosternum.
Range: South America.
Temp: 18-27°C   **Max.Size**: 20 cm.
Water: pH 6-7.5.   **Aquarium**: 100 cm.
Difficulty: 3.
Comments: Omnivorous. Eats all normal foods. Bubblenest brooder. Peaceful, but adult specimens sometimes regard smaller specimens as food.

Name: *Hypancistrus zebra*
Family: Loricariidae.
Trade name: Zebra suckermouth, zebra plec, L 46.
Range: Brazil: Rio Xingú.
Temp: 23-32°C   **Max.Size**: 10 cm.
Water: pH 7-8.   **Aquarium**: 80 cm.
Difficulty: 4.
Comments: Omnivorous. Algae-eater. Substrate (cave)brooder. Peaceful, but males are territorial towards their own kind. Nocturnal. Needs hidingplaces and a strong current in the water. Sensitive to white spot disease.

Name: *Hypostomus margaritifer*
Family: Loricariidae.
Range: Brazil: Rio Piracicaba.
Temp: 23-26°C   **Max.Size**: 17 cm.
Water: pH 6-7.5.   **Aquarium**: 120 cm.
Difficulty: 3.
Comments: Omnivorous. Algae-eater. Substrate brooder. Relatively peaceful, but males are territorial towards their own kind. Nocturnal.

Name: *Hypostomus plecostomus*
Family: Loricariidae.
Trade name: *Plecostomus*, pleco, plec.
Range: Northern South America.
Temp: 23-26°C   **Max.Size**: 50 cm.
Water: pH 6-8.   **Aquarium**: 130 cm.
Difficulty: 1.
Comments: Omnivorous. Algae-eater. Substrate (cave) brooder. Peaceful, but males are territorial towards their own kind. Crepuscular and nocturnal. Popular aquarium fish but grows larger than most people realise.

109

Name: *Hypostomus* sp. L200
Family: Loricariidae.
Trade name: Gold-yellow hypostomus, L200.
Range: Brazil.
Temp: 23-26°C   **Max.Size**: 18 cm.
Water: pH 6-7.   **Aquarium**: 100 cm.
Difficulty: 3.
Comments: Omnivorous. Eats some algae. Substrate brooder. Peaceful but males are territorial towards their own kind. Nocturnal.

Name: *Isorineloricaria spinosissima*
Family: Loricariidae.
Trade name: *Isorineloricaria festae*, spiny suckermouth catfish.
Range: Western Ecuador.
Temp: 24-28°C   **Max.Size**: 35 cm.
Water: pH 6-8.   **Aquarium**: 160 cm.
Difficulty: 3.
Comments: Omnivorous and herbivorous. Algae-eater. Substrate brooder. Shy. Peaceful, but males are rather territorial towards their own kind. Nocturnal.

Name: *Kryptopterus minor*
Family: Siluridae.
Trade name: *Kryptopterus bicirrhis*, glass catfish.
Range: Southeast Asia.
Temp: 23-27°C   **Max.Size**: 8 cm.
Water: pH 6.5-7.5. **Aquarium**: 80 cm.
Difficulty: 4.
Comments: Omnivorous. Live food, but accepts dry foods. Shoaling-fish. Daylight active. Peaceful. Sensitive.

Name: *Lamontichthys filamentosus*
Family: Loricariidae.
Trade name: Filamentosus suckermouth.
Range: Brazil, Ecuador, Bolivia, Peru.
Temp: 23-26°C   **Max.Size**: 22 cm.
Water: pH 6-7.5.   **Aquarium**: 120 cm.
Difficulty: 3.
Comments: Omnivorous. Eats some algae. Need live or frozen foods, but sometimes accepts dry foods. Substrate brooder. Peaceful, but males are somewhat territorial. Nocturnal.

Name: *Leporacanthicus galaxias*
Family: Loricariidae.
Trade name: Vampire pleco.
Range: Brazil: Amazon basin.
Temp: 23-26°C   **Max.Size**: 35 cm.
Water: pH 6-7.   **Aquarium**: 150 cm.
Difficulty: 3.
Comments: Herbivorous. Algae eater. Substrate brooder. Peaceful, but males are rather territorial and aggressive towards their own kind. Nocturnal. Needs oxygen-rich water of high quality.

Name: *Leporacanthicus heterodon*
Family: Loricariidae.
Trade name: L 172.
Range: Brazil.
Temp: 23-26°C   **Max.Size**: 25 cm.
Water: pH 6-7.   **Aquarium**: 120 cm.
Difficulty: 3.
Comments: Omnivorous. Eats some algae. Substrate brooder. Peaceful, but males are territorial towards their own kind. Nocturnal.

Name: *Liosomadoras oncinus*
Family: Auchenipteridae.
Trade name: Jaguar catfish.
Range: Peru, Brazil.
Temp: 21-25°C   **Max.Size**: 17 cm.
Water: pH 5-7.   **Aquarium**: 120 cm.
Difficulty: 3.
Comments: Carnivorous and piscivorous. Live food (fishes smaller than 4-5 cm) and frozen food. Eggs are fertilized internally. Nocturnal. Relatively peaceful. Exists in several colour patterns.

Name: *Megalancistrus gigas*
Family: Loricariidae.
Trade name: L 113.
Range: Paraguay.
Temp: 23-26°C   **Max.Size**: 25 cm.
Water: pH 6-7.5.   **Aquarium**: 150 cm.
Difficulty: 3.
Comments: Herbivorous and omnivorous. Substrate brooder. Eats some algae. Peaceful, but males are territorial towards their own kind. Nocturnal.

Mark Smith

Name: *Megalodoras irwini*
Family: Doradidae.
Range: Amazon basin.
Temp: 23-26°C   **Max.Size**: 70 cm.
Water: pH 6-7.5.   **Aquarium**: 250 cm.
Difficulty: 4.
Comments: Omnivorous. Eat fruits, snails, among others. Peaceful. Adults are too large for normal aquaria (but grows slowly).

Name: *Microglanis iheringi*
Family: Pimelodidae.
Trade name: Bumblebee catfish.
Range: Peru, Colombia, Venezuela.
Temp: 21-26°C   **Max.Size**: 8 cm.
Water: pH 6-8.   **Aquarium**: 80 cm.
Difficulty: 2.
Comments: Omnivorous. Frozen foods, but also accepts dry foods. Egg-scatterer. Nocturnal and shy. Peaceful.

Mark Smith

Name: *Otocinclus vittatus*
Family: Loricariidae.
Trade name: Striped otocinclus.
Rango: Brazil, Peru, Bolivia.
Temp: 21-25°C   **Max.Size**: 5.5 cm.
Water: pH 6-7.5.   **Aquarium**: 50 cm.
Difficulty: 3.
Comments: Omnivorous. All *Otocinlus* are splendid algae-eaters for small aquaria. Needs vegetable foods, e.g. algae, frozen green peas (thawed), and vegetable tablet foods. Substrate (plants) brooder. Peaceful.

Name: *Panaque nigrolineatus*
Family: Loricariidae.
Trade name: Royal plec.
Rango: Venezuela to southern Brazil.
Temp: 22-26°C   **Max.Size**: 60 cm.
Water: pH 6-7.5.   **Aquarium**: 160 cm.
Difficulty: 3.
Comments: Herbivorous. Algae-eater, needs a lot of algae. Can also be fed with vegetable tablet foods and frozen green peas (thawed). Peaceful. Males are territorial. Somewhat nocturnal. In nature max 60 cm, in aquarium max. 40cm.

Name: *Panaque suttoni*
Family: Loricariidae.
Trade name: *Panaque suttonorum*, blue-eyed plec.
Range: Colombia, Guyana.
Temp: 22-25°C   **Max.Size**: 45 cm.
Water: pH 6-7.5.   **Aquarium**: 150 cm.
Difficulty: 3.
Comments: Omnivorous. Algae-eater. Can also be fed with vegetable tablet foods and frozen green peas (thawed). Peaceful. Males are territorial. Somewhat nocturnal. In aquarium max. 35 cm.

Name: *Pangasius hypophthalmus*
Family: Pangasiidae.
Trade name: *Pangasius sutchii*, Shark catfish.
Range: Thailand.
Temp: 22-25°C   **Max.Size**: 130 cm.
Water: pH 6.5-7.5. **Aquarium**: 300 cm.
Difficulty: 5.
Comments: Omnivorous. Eats all normal foods. Shoaling fish. Easily scared and can injure themselves. Too big for most aquaria. Jumps. 130 cm in nature — 80 cm in aquaria.

Name: *Parancistrus aurantiacus*
Family: Loricariidae.
Range: Brazil, Peru.
Temp: 23-27°C   **Max.Size**: 18 cm.
Water: pH 6-7.5.   **Aquarium**: 120 cm.
Difficulty: 3.
Comments: Omnivorous. Eat some algae. Substrate brooder. Peaceful, but males are territorial towards their own kind. Nocturnal.

Name: *Peckoltia pulcher*
Family: Loricariidae.
Trade name: *Peckoltia pulchra*, pretty Peckoltia.
Range: Colombia, Brazil: Rio Negro.
Temp: 23-27°C   **Max.Size**: 8 cm.
Water: pH 6-7.5.   **Aquarium**: 80 cm.
Difficulty: 3.   **Comments**: Herbivorous. Eats more or less only algae, so keep no more than one fish per 60-L water, to ensure there is enough algae. Peaceful, but territorial towards its own kind. Somewhat nocturnal.

113

Name: *Peckoltia* sp. L66
Family: Loricariidae.
Trade name: King tiger pleco.
Range: Brazil: Rio Xingú.
Temp: 23-27°C   **Max.Size**: 12 cm.
Water: pH 6-7.5.   **Aquarium**: 100 cm.
Difficulty: 3.
Comments: Herbivorous. Algae-eater. Substrate brooder. Peaceful, but males are territorial towards their own kind. Somewhat nocturnal.

Name: *Peckoltia vittata*
Family: Loricariidae.
Trade name: Striped peckoltia.
Range: Brazil: Amazonas region.
Temp: 23-27°C   **Max.Size**: 14 cm.
Water: pH 5.5-7.5. **Aquarium**: 100 cm.
Difficulty: 2.
Comments: Herbivorous. Algae-eater. Eats more or less only algae, so keep no more than one fish per 60-L water, to ensure there is enough algae. Peaceful, but territorial towards its own kind. Somewhat nocturnal.

Name: *Phractocephalus hemioliopterus*
Family: Pimelodidae.
Trade name: Redtail catfish.
Range: Amazon basin.
Temp: 20-26°C   **Max.Size**: 130 cm.
Water: pH 5.5-7.   **Aquarium**: 400 cm.
Difficulty: 5.
Comments: Omnivorous and piscivorous. Eat absolutely everything, including most other fishes in the aquarium. Territorial. Grows very fast. Sold as attractive small juveniles, but rapidly too big for normal aquaria.

Name: *Pimelodus ornatus*
Family: Pimelodidae.
Trade name: Ornate pim.
Range: Peru, Surinam, Brazil.
Temp: 23-26°C   **Max.Size**: 30 cm.
Water: pH 6-7.5.   **Aquarium**: 200 cm.
Difficulty: 3.
Comments: Omnivorous. Eat small fishes (< 6cm). Egg-scatterer. Very active swimming behaviour — restless.

Name: *Pimelodus pictus*
Family: Pimelodidae.
Trade name: Angelicus pim, polka-dot catfish.
Range: Peru, Colombia.
Temp: 23-26°C   **Max.Size**: 15 cm.
Water: pH 6-7.5.   **Aquarium**: 120 cm.
Difficulty: 2.
Comments: Omnivorous. Peaceful, but may eat very small fishes. Nocturnal. Egg-scatterer. Very active swimming behaviour. Somewhat restless. Two variants are known, different spots.

Name: *Platydoras costatus*
Family: Doradidae.
Trade name: Chocolate doradid.
Range: Brazil to Peru.
Temp: 23-28°C   **Max.Size**: 22 cm.
Water: pH 6-7.5.   **Aquarium**: 120 cm.
Difficulty: 2.
Comments: Omnivorous. Piscivorous — eats small fishes. Extremely territorial towards its own kind and also quarrels with other nocturnal catfishes. Fine sand in the aquarium.

Name: *Pseudacanthicus leopardus*
Family: Loricariidae.
Trade name: Xingu-cactus catfish, L114.
Range: Brazil: Rio Negro.
Temp: 24-26°C   **Max.Size**: 30 cm.
Water: pH 6-7.5.   **Aquarium**: 200 cm.
Difficulty: 4.
Comments: Omnivorous. Eats some algae. Substrate brooder. Somewhat nocturnal. Aggressive towards its own kind.

Name: *Pseudacanthicus* sp. "Scarlet"
Family: Loricariidae.
Trade name: Scarlet cat, L25.
Range: Brazil: Rio Xingú.
Temp: 24-26°C   **Max.Size**: 35 cm.
Water: pH 6-7.5.   **Aquarium**: 200 cm.
Difficulty: 4.
Comments: Omnivorous. Algae-eater. Substrate brooder. Somewhat nocturnal. Aggressive towards its own kind.

Name: *Sciades pictus*
Family: Pimelodidae.
Trade name: *Leiarius pictus*, Sailfin pimelodid.
Range: Amazon region.
Temp: 23-26°C   **Max.Size**: 60 cm.
Water: pH 6-7.5.   **Aquarium**: 250 cm.
Difficulty: 5.
Comments: Carnivorous. Piscivorous. Eats other fishes, but also accepts large earthworms. Should be kept only with other very large fishes. Sensitive.

Name: *Scobinancistrus aureatus*
Family: Loricariidae.
Trade name: Sun suckercat, L14.
Range: Brazil: Rio Xingú.
Temp: 23-28°C   **Max.Size**: 35 cm.
Water: pH 6-7.5.   **Aquarium**: 200 cm.
Difficulty: 4.
Comments: Omnivorous. Eats some algae. Substrate brooder. Somewhat nocturnal. Aggressive towards its own kind.

Name: *Sorubim lima*
Family: Pimelodidae.
Trade name: Shovelnose catfish.
Range: South America.
Temp: 23-28°C   **Max.Size**: 60 cm.
Water: pH 6.5-8.   **Aquarium**: 200 cm.
Difficulty: 3.
Comments: Carnivorous. Piscivorous, not to be kept together with smaller fishes. Also accepts frozen food and sometimes pellets. Needs oxygen-rich water, of high quality.

Name: *Sturisoma aureum*
Family: Loricariidae.
Trade name: Giant whiptail.
Range: Colombia, Venezuela, Brazil.
Temp: 24-27°C   **Max.Size**: 30 cm.
Water: pH 6-7.5.   **Aquarium**: 120 cm.
Difficulty: 3.
Comments: Herbivorous. Algae-eater. Algae and mashed (thawed) frozen green peas necessary. Substrate (plants) brooder. Somewhat territorial towards its own kind. High water quality with good water movement required.

Name: *Synodontis angelicus*
Family: Mochokidae.
Trade name: Polka-dot Synodontis, angelicus.
Range: Congo Basin.
Temp: 23-26°C   **Max.Size**: 30 cm.
Water: pH 6-8.   **Aquarium**: 150 cm.
Difficulty: 4.
Comments: Omnivorous. Eats all normal foods. Peaceful, but semi-adult specimens can be extremely territorial. Nocturnal. Needs hiding-places. Somewhat sensitive.

Name: *Synodontis brichardi*
Family: Mochokidae.
Trade name: Brichard's Synodontis.
Range: Lower Congo River.
Temp: 23-26°C   **Max.Size**: 15 cm.
Water: pH 6-8.   **Aquarium**: 120 cm.
Difficulty: 3.
Comments: Omnivorous. Eats all normal foods. Crepuscular and nocturnal. Peaceful. Good water movement required. Needs hiding-places.

Name: *Synodontis decorus*
Family: Mochokidae.
Trade name: Clown Synodontis.
Range: Upper Congo, Cameroon.
Temp: 23-26°C   **Max.Size**: 30 cm.
Water: pH 6-8.   **Aquarium**: 150 cm.
Difficulty: 3.
Comments: Omnivorous. Eats all normal foods. Crepuscular and nocturnal. Rather peaceful. Good water movement required. Needs hiding-places.

Name: *Synodontis flavitaeniatus*
Family: Mochokidae.
Trade name: Orange-striped Synodontis.
Range: Zaire: Stanley Pool.
Temp: 23-26°C   **Max.Size**: 20 cm.
Water: pH 6-8.   **Aquarium**: 150 cm.
Difficulty: 2.
Comments: Omnivorous. Eats all normal foods. Less nocturnal than many other *Synodontis* species. Peaceful. Good water movement required. Needs hiding-places.

117

Name: *Synodontis granulosus*
Family: Mochokidae.
Trade name: Granular Synodontis.
Range: Lake Tanganyika.
Temp: 23-27°C   **Max.Size**: 27 cm.
Water: pH 7-8.5.   **Aquarium**: 200 cm.
Difficulty: 4.
Comments: Omnivorous. Eats all normal foods. Diurnal and crepuscular. Peaceful. Good water movement required. Needs hiding-places. Somewhat sensitive.

Name: *Synodontis multipunctatus*
Family: Mochokidae.
Trade name: Cuckoo Synodontis.
Range: Lake Tanganyika.
Temp: 23-27°C   **Max.Size**: 25 cm.
Water: pH 7-8.5.   **Aquarium**: 200 cm.
Difficulty: 2.
Comments: Omnivorous. Eats all normal foods. Cuckoo-breeder, substitutes eggs for those of spawning mouthbrooding cichlids. Diurnal and crepuscular. Peaceful. Best kept in small groups. Good water movement required. Needs hiding-places.

Name: *Synodontis nigriventris*
Family: Mochokidae.
Trade name: Upside-down catfish.
Range: Congo Basin.
Temp: 23-26°C   **Max.Size**: 10 cm.
Water: pH 6-7.5.   **Aquarium**: 80 cm.
Difficulty: 1.
Comments: Omnivorous. Eats all normal foods. Substrate (cave) brooder. Crepuscular and nocturnal. Peaceful. Best kept in small groups. Swims mostly upside-down. Needs hiding-places.

Name: *Synodontis njassae*
Family: Mochokidae.
Trade name: Nyassa Synodontis.
Range: Lake Malawi.
Temp: 22-25°C   **Max.Size**: 20 cm.
Water: pH 7-8.5.   **Aquarium**: 120 cm.
Difficulty: 1.
Comments: Omnivorous. Eats all normal foods. Substrate (cave) brooder. Crepuscular and nocturnal. Peaceful, but sometimes chases smaller fishes. Needs hiding-places.

118

Name: *Synodontis notatus*
Family: Mochokidae.
Trade name: Spotted Synodontis.
Range: Zaire.
Temp: 23-26°C   **Max.Size**: 20 cm.
Water: pH 6-7.5.   **Aquarium**: 120 cm.
Difficulty: 2.
Comments: Omnivorous. Eats all normal foods. Crepuscular and nocturnal. Peaceful, but semi-adults can be aggressive. Needs hiding-places.

Name: *Synodontis polli*
Family: Mochokidae.
Trade name: Poll's upside-down catfish.
Range: Lake Tanganyika.
Temp: 22-26°C   **Max.Size**: 16 cm.
Water: pH 7.5-8.5. **Aquarium**: 120 cm.
Difficulty: 2.
Comments: Omnivorous. Eats all normal foods. Possibly a cuckoo breeder. Crepuscular and nocturnal. Peaceful. Good water movement required. Needs hiding-places.

Name: *Tatia perugiae*
Family: Auchenipteridae.
Range: Colombia, Peru, Ecuador.
Temp: 24-28°C   **Max.Size**: 8 cm.
Water: pH 6-7.   **Aquarium**: 60 cm.
Difficulty: 3.
Comments: Carnivorous. Has a small mouth and therefore needs small foods. Nocturnal. Peaceful. Solitary. Needs hiding-places.

Name: *Wallago attu*
Family: Siluridae.
Trade name: Helicopter catfish.
Range: Tropical Asia.
Temp: 22-26°C   **Max.Size**: 240 cm.
Water: pH 6.5-7.5. **Aquarium**: 500 cm.
Difficulty: 5.
Comments: Omnivorous. Piscivorous, eats everything smaller than itself. Nocturnal. Jumps. Not an aquarium fish.

South American Cichlids

South America is a big continent and here are found many of the of most common aquarium fishes, for example the neon and cardinal tetras. Here too are found many beautiful and interesting cichlid species that have become popular in the aquarium hobby, for example angels, discus, and the South American butterfly cichlid (*Mikrogeophagus ramirezi*) to mention but a few. The most important area for cichlids is the gigantic Amazon basin, but the cichlids are only very rarely found in the open water of large rivers. Hence most of the cichlids instead live in creeks, pools, and lakes, and for part of the year in the flooded forest. In these habitats they prefer mainly to hide among roots and dead wood or in the leaf litter on the bottom.

In South America there is a broad spectrum of cichlids, ranging from the small dwarf cichlids (e.g. *Apistogramma* species) through majestic angels and discus (the latter is sometimes called the king of aquarium fishes) to gigantic Oscars (*Astronotus ocellatus*), and it should be self-evident that it isn't possible to mix such different fishes, even if they all are cichlids and are all from South America. The same rules apply here as for all other aquarium fishes (apart from rare exceptions): don't mix big fishes with small fishes and don't keep predators together with smaller species.

The decor of an aquarium for South American cichlids will depend on what species you wish to keep. An aquarium for Oscars can be decorated only with large pieces of wood and rock since they will move anything else in the aquarium. The so-called earth-eaters (*Geophagus* species, etc.) are usually a lot easier to keep in the aquarium, even though they too grow relatively big, but since they "sift" the gravel the latter must be fine-grained (max. 2 mm). The dwarf cichlids are most often kept mixed with different tetras and catfishes and can readily be maintained in a aquarium that contains plants, some wood, and small rocks which should be used to create a number of caves.

The water in South America is mainly soft and acid to neutral (pH 5-7) but varies somewhat depending on geographical and seasonal variations. The temperature generally varies between 24-30°C. In an aquarium that contains South American fishes the temperature should be 25-27°C and the pH 6.5-7 for the majority of species. A pH above 7.5 is generally totally unsuitable. Most of the South American cichlids are substrate brooders (see BREEDING) although there are also some mouthbrooding species. It is often impossible to detect any sexual dimorphism in juveniles, or even in adults of many species, and because of this it is better to buy a small group of each species and let them form pairs naturally. South American cichlids are unproblematical as regards food. Flake food or high quality granular food combined with frozen foods such as *Cyclops*, glassworm, and mosquito larvae, is appreciated (see FOOD).

Name: *Acarichthys heckelii*
Family: Cichlidae.
Trade name: Threadfin acara.
Range: North-eastern South America.
Temp: 22-27°C.   **Max.Size**: 22 cm.
Water: pH 6.0-7.0 **Aquarium**: 150 cm.
Difficulty: 3.
Comments: Omnivorous. Live foods, but once acclimated will take other foods. Territorial, but relative peaceful. Pairing fish. Substrate (cave) brooder.

Name: *Aequidens pulcher*
Family: Cichlidae.
Trade name: *Aequidens latifrons*, Blue acara.
Range: Trinidad, Venezuela, Colombia.
Temp: 22-25°C.   **Max.Size**: 20 cm.
Water: pH 6.8-7.5 **Aquarium**: 100 cm.
Difficulty: 2.
Comments: Carnivorous and omnivorous. Live and frozen foods. Also takes dry foods. Territorial, and somewhat aggressive. Pairing fish. Open substrate brooder.

Name: *Aequidens rivulatus*
Family: Cichlidae.
Trade name: Green terror, Gold saum.
Range: Western Ecuador.
Temp: 20-25°C.   **Max.Size**: 25 cm.
Water: pH 6.5-7.5 **Aquarium**: 120 cm.
Difficulty: 3.
Comments: Carnivorous and omnivorous. Eats all normal foods. Territorial and aggressive. Pairing fish. Open substrate brooder.

Name: *Apistogramma agassizii*
Family: Cichlidae.
Range: Peru, Brazil.
Temp: 25-27°C.   **Max.Size**: 8 cm.
Water: pH 5.0-6.5. **Aquarium**: 80 cm.
Difficulty: 3.
Comments: Carnivorous and omnivorous. Small live foods combined with dry/frozen foods. Territorial. Peaceful. Substrate (cave) brooder. If more than one male, larger aquarium is necessary. Needs hiding-places and dense planting.

Name: *Apistogramma bitaeniata*
Family: Cichlidae.
Trade name: Two-banded dwarf cichlid.
Range: Peru, Colombia, Brazil.
Temp: 24-27°C.   **Max.Size**: 7 cm.
Water: pH 5.5-7.0. **Aquarium**: 60 cm.
Difficulty: 3.
Comments: Carnivorous and omnivorous. Small live foods combined with frozen/dry foods. Territorial. Peaceful. Substrate (cave) brooder. If more than one male, larger aquarium is necessary. Needs hiding-places and dense planting.

Name: *Apistogramma borelli*
Family: Cichlidae.
Trade name: Borelli´s dwarf cichlid.
Range: Brazil: Matto Grosso, Rio Paraguay.
Temp: 24-26°C.   **Max.Size**: 7 cm.
Water: pH 6.0-7.0. **Aquarium**: 60 cm.
Difficulty: 3.   **Comments**: Omnivorous. Small live foods combined with frozen/dry foods. Territorial. Peaceful. Cave brooder. If more than one male, larger aquarium is necessary. Needs hiding-places and dense planting.

Name: *Apistogramma cacatuoides*
Family: Cichlidae.
Trade name: Cockatoo dwarf cichlid.
Range: Peru, Brazil.
Temp: 24-26°C.   **Max.Size**: 7 cm.
Water: pH 6.0-7.5. **Aquarium**: 60 cm.
Difficulty: 2.
Comments: Carnivorous and omnivorous. Small live foods combined with frozen/dry foods. Territorial. Peaceful. Substrate (cave) brooder. If more than one male, larger aquarium is necessary. Needs hiding-places and dense planting.

Name: *Apistogramma hongsloi*
Family: Cichlidae.
Trade name: Redlined dwarf cichlid.
Range: Venezuela, Colombia.
Temp: 24-27°C.   **Max.Size**: 8 cm.
Water: pH 5.0-6.5. **Aquarium**: 80 cm.
Difficulty: 3.
Comments: Carnivorous. Small live foods. Sometimes accepts dry/frozen foods. Territorial. Peaceful. Substrate (cave) brooder. If more than one male, larger aquarium is necessary. Needs hiding-places and dense planting.

Name: *Apistogramma nijsseni*
Family: Cichlidae.
Trade name: Panda dwarf cichlid.
Range: Peru: Rio Ucayalii drainage.
Temp: 24-27°C.   **Max.Size**: 9 cm.
Water: pH 5.0-6.5. **Aquarium**: 100 cm.
Difficulty: 3.
Comments: Carnivorous. Small live foods. Sometimes accepts dry/frozen foods. Territorial. Peaceful. Substrate (cave) brooder. If more than one male, larger aquarium is necessary. Needs hiding-places and dense planting.

Name: *Apistogramma panduro*
Family: Cichlidae.
Trade name: Azure dwarf cichlid, pandurini.
Range: Peru: Rio Ucayali drainage.
Temp: 24-27°C.   **Max.Size**: 8 cm.
Water: pH 5.5-7.0. **Aquarium**: 60 cm.
Difficulty: 3.   **Comments**: Omnivorous. Small live foods. Sometimes accepts dry/frozen foods. Territorial. Peaceful. Substrate (cave) brooder. If more than one male, larger aquarium is necessary. Needs hiding-places and dense planting.

Name: *Apistogramma pertensis*
Family: Cichlidae.
Range: Central Amazon river.
Temp: 23-28°C.   **Max.Size**: 7 cm.
Water: pH 5.0-6.0. **Aquarium**: 60 cm.
Difficulty: 4.
Comments: Carnivorous. Small live foods. Sometimes accepts dry/frozen foods. Territorial. Peaceful. Substrate (cave) brooder. If more than one male, larger aquarium is necessary. Needs hiding-places and dense planting.

Name: *Apistogramma viejita*
Family: Cichlidae.
Trade name: Viejita dwarf cichlid.
Range: Colombia: Rio Meta drainage
Temp: 24-27°C.   **Max.Size**: 8 cm.
Water: pH 5.5-6.5. **Aquarium**: 60 cm.
Difficulty: 4.
Comments: Carnivorous. Small live foods. Sometimes accepts dry/frozen foods. Territorial. Peaceful. Substrate (cave) brooder. If more than one male, larger aquarium is necessary. Needs hiding-places and dense planting.

Name: *Astronotus ocellatus*
Family: Cichlidae.
Trade name: Oscar; peacock cichlid.
Range: Amazonas basin.
Temp: 24-26°C.   **Max.Size**: 40 cm.
Water: pH 6.0-8.0. **Aquarium**: 160 cm.
Difficulty: 3.   **Comments**: Carnivorous, partly piscivorous. Greedy eater. Very aggressive when breeding. Open spawner. The Oscar's are often sold in petshops as "babies", but they grow very quickly. Exists in several aquarium strains. Digs a lot.

Name: *Biotodoma cupido*
Family: Cichlidae.
Trade name: Cupid cichlid.
Range: Guyana to Amazon basin.
Temp: 23-26°C.   **Max.Size**: 13 cm.
Water: pH 6.0-7.5. **Aquarium**: 100 cm.
Difficulty: 3.
Comments: Carnivorous. Small live food. Sometimes accepts dry/frozen foods. When breeding very territorial and aggressive. Pairing fish or harem-forming fish. Open substrate brooder. Needs hiding-places.

Name: *Biotodoma wavrini*
Family: Cichlidae.
Trade name: Orinoco eartheater.
Range: North-eastern South America.
Temp: 24-28°C.   **Max.Size**: 15 cm.
Water: pH 6.0-7.0. **Aquarium**: 100 cm.
Difficulty: 3.
Comments: Carnivorous. Small live food. Sometimes accepts dry/frozen foods. Territorial when breeding. Peaceful. Shy. Pairing fish or harem-forming fish. Open substrate brooder. Needs hiding-places.

Name: *Cichla ocellaris*
Family: Cichlidae.
Trade name: Peacock bass.
Range: Tropical South America.
Temp: 24-27°C.   **Max.Size**: 90 cm.
Water: pH 6.0-8.0. **Aquarium**: 250 cm.
Difficulty: 5.
Comments: Carnivorous. Piscivorous. Eat all kinds of live foods. Territorial, but peaceful for its size. Open spawner. Needs hiding-places. Possibly the biggest cichlid in the world. Too big for most aquaria.

Name: *'Cichlasoma' festae*
Family: Cichlidae.
Trade name: Red terror.
Range: Western Ecuador.
Temp: 23-28°C.   **Max.Size**: 50 cm.
Water: pH 6.5-7.5. **Aquarium**: 200 cm.
Difficulty: 4.
Comments: Carnivorous and omnivorous. Piscivorous. Eat all kinds of live foods. Territorial and very aggressive. Open substrate brooder. Digs a lot. Needs hiding-places and a very large aquarium.

Name: *Cleithracara maronii*
Family: Cichlidae.
Trade name: Keyhole cichlid.
Range: Guyana, Guiana, Surinam.
Temp: 24-26°C.   **Max.Size**: 15 cm.
Water: pH 6.5-7.0. **Aquarium**: 80 cm.
Difficulty: 2.
Comments: Carnivorous and omnivorous. Eats all normal foods. Peaceful. Pairing fish. Open substrate brooder. Needs hiding-places. Good fish for community aquaria.

Name: *Crenicichla compressiceps*
Family: Cichlidae.
Range: Brazil: Tocantins, Araguaia.
Temp: 24-26°C.   **Max.Size**: 8 cm.
Water: pH 6.0-7.0. **Aquarium**: 80 cm.
Difficulty: 3.
Comments: Carnivorous and omnivorous. Piscovorous, eats very small fishes. Small live and frozen foods. Substrate (cave) brooder. Needs hiding-places. Strongly territorial. Do not keep with very small fishes.

Name: *Crenicichla regani*
Family: Cichlidae.
Trade name: Regan´s pike cichlid.
Range: Brazil.
Temp: 24-26°C.   **Max.Size**: 14 cm.
Water: pH 5.5-6.5. **Aquarium**: 120 cm.
Difficulty: 3.
Comments: Carnivorous. Partly piscivorous, eats small fishes. Small live and frozen foods. Cave brooder. Pairing fish. Needs hiding-places. Strongly territorial. Do not keep with small fishes.

Name: *Crenicichla* sp. Xingu I
Family: Cichlidae.
Range: Brazil: Rio Xingu.
Temp: 24-26°C.   **Max.Size**: 40 cm.
Water: pH 5.5-7.0. **Aquarium**: 200 cm.
Difficulty: 4.
Comments: Carnivorous. Piscivorous, eats fishes. Substrate (cave) brooder. Pairing fish. Needs hiding-places. Territorial and aggressive. Keep only together with other large fishes.

Name: *Dicrossus filamentosus*
Family: Cichlidae.
Trade name: Checkerboard cichlid, *Crenicara filamentosa*.
Range: Northwestern Brazil.
Temp: 25-28°C.   **Max.Size**: 9 cm.
Water: pH 4.5-6.0. **Aquarium**: 80 cm.
Difficulty: 4.
Comments: Carnivorous. Small live and frozen foods. Substrate (cave) brooder. Needs hiding-places. Territorial. Delicate, sensitive fish.

Name: *Geophagus brasiliensis*
Family: Cichlidae.
Trade name: Pearl cichlid, Brazilian eartheater.
Range: Eastern and southern Brazil.
Temp: 20-25°C.   **Max.Size**: 30 cm.
Water: pH 6.0-7.0. **Aquarium**: 150 cm.
Difficulty: 3.   **Comments**: Omnivorous. Small live and frozen foods, but also dry food. Open spawner. Needs hiding-places. Territorial and somewhat aggressive. Pairing fish. Needs fine sand (max. 2mm) on the bottom.

Name: *Geophagus pellegrini*
Family: Cichlidae.
Trade name: Yellow hump eartheater.
Range: Colombia.
Temp: 24-28°C.   **Max.Size**: 18 cm.
Water: pH 6.5-7.5. **Aquarium**: 130 cm.
Difficulty: 2.
Comments: Carnivorous and omnivorous. Small live and frozen foods, but also dry foods. Mouth brooder. Territorial when breeding. Peaceful. Only male has hump. Needs fine sand (max. 2mm) on the bottom.

Name: *Geophagus steindachneri*
Family: Cichlidae.
Trade name: *G. hondae*, Redhump geophagus.
Range: Colombia, Venezuela.
Temp: 23-26°C.   **Max.Size**: 25 cm.
Water: pH 7.0-7.5. **Aquarium**: 130 cm.
Difficulty: 2.   **Comments**: Omnivorous. Small live and frozen foods, but also dry foods. Mouth brooder. Territorial when breeding. Peaceful. Only male has hump. Needs fine sand (max. 2mm) on the bottom.

127

Name: *Geophagus surinamensis*
Family: Cichlidae.
Trade name: Red striped eartheater.
Range: Surinam.
Temp: 24-27°C.　**Max.Size**: 25 cm.
Water: pH 6.0-7.5. **Aquarium**: 160 cm.
Difficulty: 3.
Comments: Carnivorous and omnivorous. Small live and frozen foods, but also dry foods. Substrate brooder or partly mouth brooder. Territorial when breeding. Peaceful. Shoaling fish. Needs fine sand (max. 2mm) on the bottom.

Name: *Guianacara cf. geayi*
Family: Cichlidae.
Trade name: Red-cheek Guianacara.
Range: Northern Amazon-region incl. Guianas.
Temp: 24-28°C.　**Max.Size**: 15 cm.
Water: pH 6.0-7.5. **Aquarium**: 120 cm.
Difficulty: 3.
Comments: Omnivorous. Small live and frozen foods, but also dry foods. Substrate (cave) brooder. Peaceful. Pairing fish. Needs hiding-places.

Name: *Gymnogeophagus gymnogenys*
Family: Cichlidae.
Range: Southern Brazil to Uruguay.
Temp: 20-24°C.　**Max.Size**: 25 cm.
Water: pH 6.5-7.5. **Aquarium**: 120 cm.
Difficulty: 3.
Comments: Omnivorous. Small live and frozen foods, but also dry foods. Open spawner. Partly mouthbrooder. Needs hiding-places. Territorial, but relative peaceful. Needs fine sand (max. 2mm) on the bottom.

Name: *Gymnogeophagus rhabdotus*
Family: Cichlidae.
Range: South Brazil, Uruguay, Argentina.
Temp: 20-24°C.　**Max.Size**: 15 cm.
Water: pH 6.5-7.5. **Aquarium**: 100 cm.
Difficulty: 3.
Comments: Omnivorous. Small live and frozen foods, but also dry foods. Open substrate brooder. Needs hiding-places. Territorial but relative peaceful. Pairing fish. Needs fine sand (max. 2mm) on the bottom

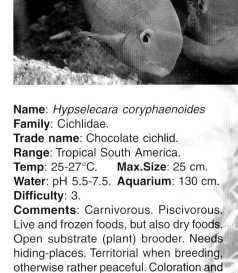

Name: *Heros appendiculatus*
Family: Cichlidae.
Trade name: Severum, Deacon.
Range: Amazon basin.
Temp: 24-26°C.   **Max.Size**: 30 cm.
Water: pH 5.5-7.5. **Aquarium**: 150 cm.
Difficulty: 2.
Comments: Omnivorous. Live and frozen foods, but also dry foods with vegetable content. Open substrate (plant) brooder. Pairing fish. Needs hiding-places. Territorial when breeding, otherwise rather peaceful.

Name: *Hypselecara coryphaenoides*
Family: Cichlidae.
Trade name: Chocolate cichlid.
Range: Tropical South America.
Temp: 25-27°C.   **Max.Size**: 25 cm.
Water: pH 5.5-7.5. **Aquarium**: 130 cm.
Difficulty: 3.
Comments: Carnivorous. Piscivorous. Live and frozen foods, but also dry foods. Open substrate (plant) brooder. Needs hiding-places. Territorial when breeding, otherwise rather peaceful. Coloration and pattern variable.

Name: *Krobia guianensis*
Family: Cichlidae.
Range: Guyana, Surinam.
Temp: 24-26°C.   **Max.Size**: 13 cm.
Water: pH 6.0-7.0. **Aquarium**: 80 cm.
Difficulty: 3.
Comments: Carnivorous and omnivorous. Live and frozen foods, but also dry foods Open substrate brooder. Needs hiding-places. Territorial, but not too aggressive.

Name: *Laetacara curviceps*
Family: Cichlidae.
Trade name: *Aequidens curviceps*.
Range: Amazon region.
Temp: 24-27°C.   **Max.Size**: 10 cm.
Water: pH 6.5-7.5. **Aquarium**: 80 cm.
Difficulty: 2.
Comments: Carnivorous and omnivorous. Small live and frozen foods, but also dry foods. Pairing fish. Open spawner. Needs hiding-places. Pairing fish. Territorial and somewhat aggressive when breeding, otherwise peaceful.

129

Name: *Mesonauta insignis*
Family: Cichlidae.
Trade name: Festivum, flag cichlid.
Range: Western Guyana, Brazil.
Temp: 24-28°C.   Max.Size: 20 cm.
Water: pH 5.5-7.5. Aquarium: 120 cm.
Difficulty: 2.
Comments: Carnivorous and omnivorous. Live and frozen foods, but also dry foods with vegetable content. Open substrate (plant) brooder. Needs hiding-places. Pairing fish. Territorial, but peaceful.

Name: *Mikrogeophagus altispinosus*
Family: Cichlidae.
Trade name: Bolivian ram.
Range: Bolivia.
Temp: 24-26°C.   Max.Size: 10 cm.
Water: pH 6.5-7.5. Aquarium: 80 cm.
Difficulty: 2.
Comments: Carnivorous and omnivorous. Small live and frozen foods, but also dry foods. Open substrate brooder. Needs hiding-places. Pairing fish. Territorial, but peaceful.

Name: *Mikrogeophagus ramirezi*
Family: Cichlidae.
Trade name: Ram, Butterfly cichlid.
Range: Venezuela, Colombia.
Temp: 25-27°C.   Max.Size: 7 cm.
Water: pH 5.5-6.5. Aquarium: 60 cm.
Difficulty: 3.
Comments: Carnivorous and omnivorous. Small live and frozen foods, but also dry foods. Open substrate brooder. Needs hiding-places. Pairing fish. Territorial, but peaceful. Very popular aquarium fish. Sensitive.

Name: *Nannacara anomala*
Family: Cichlidae.
Range: Guyana, Surinam.
Temp: 24-26°C.   Max.Size: 8 cm.
Water: pH 6.0-7.0. Aquarium: 60 cm.
Difficulty: 2.
Comments: Carnivorous. Small live and frozen foods, but also dry foods. Substrate (cave) brooder. Needs hiding-places. Pairing fish. Territorial when breeding, but rather peaceful.

Name: *Pterophyllum scalare*
Family: Cichlidae. **Trade name**: Angelfish, Scalare.
Range: Guyana to Amazon basin.
Temp: 24-26°C.   **Max.Size**: 16 cm.
Water: pH 6.0-7.5. **Aquarium**: 120 cm.
Difficulty: 2.   **Comments**: See *Pt. altum*, but *Pt. scalare* is much easier to breed. Both *Pt. altum* and *Pt. scalare* need deep aquaria, min. 45 cm-scalare, 60cm-altum. Several aquarium strains exist, including "Marbled" and "Ghost".

Name: *Pterophyllum altum*
Family: Cichlidae.
Trade name: Altum angel.
Range: Rio Orinoco, Rio Negro.
Temp: 24-26°C.   **Max.Size**: 18 cm, up to 30cm high.
Water: pH 4.5-6.0. **Aquarium**: 120 cm.
Difficulty: 3.   **Comments**: Carnivorous. Small live and frozen foods, also dry foods. Substrate (plants) brooder. Somewhat territorial. Shoaling fish when young, adults pairforming. Planted aquaria. Extremely difficult to breed.

Name: *Retroculus lapidifer*
Family: Cichlidae.
Range: Brazil.
Temp: 23-28°C.   **Max.Size**: 25 cm.
Water: pH 6.0-7.5. **Aquarium**: 150 cm.
Difficulty: 3.
Comments: Carnivorous and omnivorous. Live and frozen foods, but also dry foods. Territorial when breeding. Has a partially reduced swim bladder. Needs fine sand and small pebbles (for nest building) and good water movement.

131

Ad Konings

Name: *Satanoperca leucosticta*
Family: Cichlidae.
Trade name: *S. jurupari.*
Range: Brazil, Guyana, Surinam.
Temp: 25-28°C.　　**Max.Size**: 20 cm.
Water: pH 6.0-7.0. **Aquarium**: 120 cm.
Difficulty: 3.
Comments: Carnivorous and Omnivorous. Live and frozen foods, but also dry foods. Partly mouthbrooder. Keep in groups, breeds in pairs. Territorial when breeding. Peaceful. Needs fine sand on the bottom.

Name: *Uaru amphiacanthoides*
Family: Cichlidae.
Trade name: Triangle cichlid.
Range: Brazil, Venezuela.
Temp: 24-27°C.　　**Max.Size**: 40 cm.
Water: pH 5.5-7.0. **Aquarium**: 200 cm.
Difficulty: 3.
Comments: Omnivorous. Eat plants. Live and frozen foods, but also dry foods. Open substrate brooder. Shoaling fish (4-6). Pairs too breed. Males are territorial when breeding, otherwise peaceful. Needs hiding-places. Jumps.

Dick Au

Name: *Symphysodon aequifasciatus*
Family: Cichlidae.
Trade name: Discus, Pompadour.
Range: Amazon.
Temp: 26-29°C.　　**Max.Size**: 20 cm.
Water: pH 6.0-7.0. **Aquarium**: 120 cm.
Difficulty: 3.
Comments: Carnivorous. Small live and frozen foods, but also dry foods. Open substrate (plants) brooder. Needs hiding-places. Territorial when breeding, otherwise a shoaling fish. Occurs in several natural colour variants, but also in numerous aquarium strains. Very popular.

132

Central American Cichlids

Most of the Central American cichlids are relatively big fishes and therefore should be kept only in special aquaria. An aquarium for Central American cichlids must contain hiding-places created with rocks and/or wood, with a substrate of coarse sand or fine-grained gravel. It is better to start with a group with young fishes (5-8) and grow them up together.

Many aquarists believe that the waters of Central America are acid and soft like those of much of South America. This is wrong in most cases. In Central America the water usually has a pH between 7 and 9 and a hardness of over 10 dGH, occasionally more than 100!!. An aquarium for Central American cichlids must therefore have a pH of at least 7.

Central American cichlids will eat most foods without problems and can be fed on flake food and/ or high quality pellets (see FOOD) and frozen foods such as mysis and krill.

All Central American cichlids are substrate brooders (see BREEDING) and often produce big broods (100-1000 fry).

Name: *Amphilophus citrinellus*
Family: Cichlidae
Trade name: *Cichlasoma citrinellum*, Yellow devil, Midas cichlid.
Range: Mexico, Nicaragua, Costa Rica, Honduras
Temp: 22-26°C **Max.Size**: 30 cm
Water: pH 7-8 **Aquarium**: 200 cm
Difficulty: 3 **Comments**: Omnivorous. Eats all normal foods. Open substrate brooder. Pairing fish. Territorial. Very aggressive when breeding. Digs a lot. Needs fine sand as substrate.

Name: *Archocentrus centrarchus*
Family: Cichlidae
Trade name: *Cichlasoma centrarchus.*
Range: Nicaragua, Costa Rica, Honduras.
Temp: 23-26°C **Max.Size**: 20 cm
Water: pH 7-8 **Aquarium**: 110 cm
Difficulty: 3
Comments: Omnivorous. Eats all normal foods. Open substrate (leaves) brooder. Pairing fish. Territorial. Aggressive when breeding.

Name: *Archocentrus nigrofasciatus*
Family: Cichlidae
Trade name: *Cichlasoma nigrofasciatum*, Convict cichlid.
Range: Central America
Temp: 22-26°C **Max.Size**: 15 cm
Water: pH 7-8 **Aquarium**: 150 cm
Difficulty: 3 **Comments**: Omnivorous. Eats all normal foods. Substrate (cave) brooder. Pairing fish. Territorial and aggressive. Needs hiding-places. The albino variant is an aquarium strain. Sometimes poor quality caused by inbreeding.

Name: *Archocentrus sajica*
Family: Cichlidae
Trade name: *Cichlasoma sajica*, T-bar cichlid.
Range: Costa Rica
Temp: 22-26°C **Max.Size**: 12 cm
Water: pH 7-8 **Aquarium**: 100 cm
Difficulty: 2
Comments: Omnivorous. Eats all normal foods. Substrate (cave) brooder. Pairing fish. Territorial, but relatively peaceful. Digs a bit. Needs hiding-places.

Name: *Archocentrus septemfasciatus*
Family: Cichlidae
Trade name: *Cichlasoma septemfasciatum*.
Range: Costa Rica, Nicaragua, Panama.
Temp: 23-26°C **Max.Size**: 10 cm
Water: pH 7-8 **Aquarium**: 100 cm
Difficulty: 3 **Comments**: Omnivorous. Eats all normal foods. Substrate (cave) brooder. Pairing fish. Territorial, but relatively peaceful. Needs hiding-places. Exists in several colour variants. Needs fine sand as substrate.

Name: *Astatheros alfari*
Family: Cichlidae
Trade name: *Cichlasoma alfari*.
Range: Honduras to Panama.
Temp: 23-26°C **Max.Size**: 20 cm
Water: pH 7-8 **Aquarium**: 160 cm
Difficulty: 3
Comments: Omnivorous. Eats all normal foods. Open substrate brooder. Pairing fish. Territorial and somewhat aggressive. Needs hiding-places. Digs a lot. Extremely variable species regarding both body shape and colour.

135

Name: *Herichthys cyanoguttatus*
Family: Cichlidae
Trade name: *Cichlasoma cyanoguttatum*,
Texas cichlid.
Range: Mexico, Texas.
Temp: 20-25°C   **Max.Size**: 25 cm
Water: pH 7-8   **Aquarium**: 200 cm
Difficulty: 3
Comments: Omnivorous and herbivorous. Eats all normal foods, and plants.
Open substrate brooder. Pairing fish. Territorial and very aggressive. Needs hiding-places. Digs a lot.

Name: *Herotilapia multispinosa*
Family: Cichlidae
Trade name: Rainbow cichlid.
Range: Honduras to Costa Rica.
Temp: 22-26°C   **Max.Size**: 17 cm
Water: pH 7-8   **Aquarium**: 100 cm
Difficulty: 2
Comments: Omnivorous and carnivorous. Eats all normal foods. Open substrate brooder. Pairing fish. Territorial and
somewhat aggressive when breeding.
Needs hiding-places. Digs a bit.

Name: *Hypsophrys nicaraguensis*
Family: Cichlidae
Trade name: *Cichlasoma nicaraguense,
Copora nicaraguensis,* Spilotum.
Range: Nicaragua, Costa Rica
Temp: 22-26°C   **Max.Size**: 25 cm
Water: pH 7-8   **Aquarium**: 150 cm
Difficulty: 2
Comments: Omnivorous. Eats all normal
foods, and soft-leafed plants. Substrate
(caves, pits) brooder. Pairing fish. Territorial. Relative peaceful. Digs at spawning time. Needs hiding-places.

Name: *Nandopsis tetracanthus*
Family: Cichlidae
Trade name: *Cichlasoma tetracanthus*,
Cuban cichlid.
Range: Cuba.
Temp: 22-26°C   **Max.Size**: 25 cm
Water: pH 7-8   **Aquarium**: 200 cm
Difficulty: 2
Comments: Omnivorous and carnivorous. Eats all normal foods. Open substrate brooder. Pairing fish. Territorial, but
not so aggressive. Needs hiding-places.

136

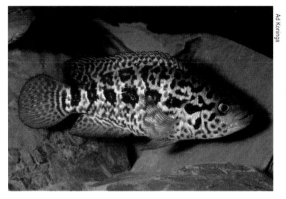

Name: *Parachromis managuensis*
Family: Cichlidae
Trade name: *Cichlasoma managuensis*, Mannie, Jaguar cichlid.
Range: Costa Rica to Honduras.
Temp: 22-26°C   **Max.Size**: 50 cm
Water: pH 7-8   **Aquarium**: 300 cm
Difficulty: 4
Comments: Omnivorous and carnivorous (piscivorous). Eats all normal foods, and fishes. Open substrate brooder. Pairing fish. Very territorial and aggressive. Digs a lot. Needs hiding-places.

Name: *Parachromis octofasciatum*
Family: Cichlidae
Trade name: *Cichlasoma octofasciatum*, Jack Dempsey.
Range: Mexico, Guatemala, Honduras.
Temp: 22-26°C   **Max.Size**: 20 cm
Water: pH 6.5-7.5 **Aquarium**: 200 cm
Difficulty: 3
Comments: Omnivorous and carnivorous (piscivorous). Eats all normal foods, and small fishes. Open substrate brooder. Pairing fish. Territorial and aggressive. Digs a lot. Needs hiding-places.

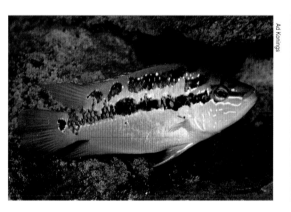

Name: *Parachromis salvini*
Family: Cichlidae
Trade name: *Cichlasoma salvini*, Salvin´s cichlid.
Range: Mexico to Guatemala.
Temp: 22-26°C   **Max.Size**: 25 cm
Water: pH 7-8   **Aquarium**: 200 cm
Difficulty: 2
Comments: Omnivorous and carnivorous. Eats all normal foods. Open substrate brooder. Pairing fish. Territorial and aggressive. Needs hiding-places.

Name: *Paratheraps synspilum*
Family: Cichlidae
Trade name: *Cichlasoma synspilum*, Synspilum, Quetzal cichlid, *Theraps synspilum*.
Range: Guatemala, Belize, Mexico.
Temp: 23-27°C   **Max.Size**: 35 cm
Water: pH 7-8   **Aquarium**: 200 cm
Difficulty: 3   **Comments**: Herbivorous. Eats all normal foods, and plants. Open substrate brooder. Pairing fish. Territorial and aggressive when breeding. Digs a lot. Needs hiding-places.

Name: *Theraps coeruleus*
Family: Cichlidae
Range: Mexico.
Temp: 23-27°C   **Max.Size**: 14 cm
Water: pH 7-8   **Aquarium**: 120 cm
Difficulty: 3
Comments: Carnivorous. Eats all normal foods. Substrate (cave) brooder. Pairing fish. Relatively peaceful. Lives in rapids, so good water movement/oxygenation needed. Needs hiding-places.

Name: *Theraps irregularis*
Family: Cichlidae
Range: Mexico, Guatemala.
Temp: 24-27°C   **Max.Size**: 25 cm
Water: pH 7-8   **Aquarium**: 200 cm
Difficulty: 4
Comments: Carnivorous. Eats all normal foods. Substrate (cave) brooder. Pairing fish. Relatively peaceful. Lives in rapids, so good water movement/oxygenation needed. Needs hiding-places.

Name: *Thorichthys aureus*
Family: Cichlidae
Range: Belize, Guatemala.
Temp: 24-27°C   **Max.Size**: 16 cm
Water: pH 7.5-8   **Aquarium**: 110 cm
Difficulty: 3
Comments: Carnivorous. Eats all normal foods. Open substrate brooder. Keep a small group. Pairing fish. Territorial, but relatively peaceful. Needs hiding-places. Needs fine sand as substrate. Exists in several colour variants.

Name: *Thorichthys helleri*
Family: Cichlidae
Range: Mexico, Guatemala.
Temp: 23-26°C   **Max.Size**: 16 cm
Water: pH 7.5-8   **Aquarium**: 100 cm
Difficulty: 2
Comments: Carnivorous and omnivorous. Eats all normal foods. Open (and cave) substrate brooder. Keep a small group. Pairing fish. Territorial, but relatively peaceful. Needs fine sand as substrate. Needs hiding-places.

Name: *Thorichthys maculipinnis*
Family: Cichlidae
Trade name: *Cichlasoma ellioti.*
Range: Mexico.
Temp: 24-27°C   **Max.Size**: 15 cm
Water: pH 7.5-8   **Aquarium**: 100 cm
Difficulty: 3
Comments: Carnivorous and omnivorous. Eats all normal foods. Open (and cave) substrate brooder. Keep a small group. Pairing fish. Territorial and somewhat aggressive. Needs fine sand as substrate. Needs hiding-places.

Name: *Thorichthys meeki*
Family: Cichlidae
Trade name: Firemouth cichlid.
Range: Mexico, Guatemala, Belize.
Temp: 23-25°C   **Max.Size**: 17 cm
Water: pH 7-8   **Aquarium**: 100 cm
Difficulty: 2
Comments: Omnivorous. Eats all normal foods. Open substrate brooder. Keep a small group. Pairing fish. Territorial and aggressive. Digs a lot. Needs fine sand as substrate. Needs hiding-places.

Name: *Vieja maculicauda*
Family: Cichlidae
Trade name: *Cichlasoma maculicauda*, Blackbelt cichlid.
Range: Belize to Panama.
Temp: 23-27°C   **Max.Size**: 30 cm
Water: pH 7-8   **Aquarium**: 300 cm
Difficulty: 4   **Comments**: Omnivorous. Eats all normal foods, and plants. Open substrate brooder. Pairing fish. Territorial and aggressive when breeding. Digs a bit. Needs hiding-places. Exists in several colour variants.

Name: *Vieja panamensis*
Family: Cichlidae
Trade name: *Cichlasoma panamense.*
Range: Panama.
Temp: 23-27°C   **Max.Size**: 13 cm
Water: pH 7-8   **Aquarium**: 100 cm
Difficulty: 3
Comments: Omnivorous. Eats all normal foods. Substrate (cave) brooder. Pairing fish. Somewhat territorial and aggressive when breeding. Needs hiding-places. Exists in several colour variants.

Malawi Cichlids

Lake Malawi, or Lake Nyassa as it is sometimes is called, is the ninth biggest lake in the world and lies in east Africa. This huge, deep (700 metres), lake is home to a lot of species that have become very popular in the aquarium hobby, mostly cichlids, and because of their beautiful colours. In fact today we recognise more than 650 different cichlid species in the lake, and almost all of them are endemic (exists in just one location) to Lake Malawi. On the following pages we will catalogue some of the most common species in the trade.

The water in Lake Malawi is alkaline (pH 7.7-8.6). Malawi cichlids are fairly robust fishes and they have a relative wide tolerance regarding the pH of the aquarium water, but the latter should always be above 7.5, and the temperature a consistent 24-26°C.

The cichlids of Lake Malawi are mouthbrooders, which means that after spawning the female takes the eggs into her mouth and then broods them for approximately 3-4 weeks, after which the by then fully-developed fry are released. They are easy to breed, and many fry will usually survive in the aquarium assuming that there are hiding-places for them.

There are only a few species of plants in Lake Malawi, and if you want to grow plants in a Malawi aquarium hardy plants as *Vallis-neria, Anubias, Crinum*, and *Ceratophyllum* are necessary. In general, however, it is not usual to have plants in a Malawi aquarium, instead the tank is decorated with rocks that provide hiding-places for the fry and where males can hold a territory.

Malawi cichlids are fairly aggressive fishes (territorial) and hence need a large aquarium (at least 150 litres for the smallest species). There will be less fighting in the aquarium if you have fewer species, but relatively many of each species. It is also an advantage if you can have more females than males in the aquarium. Normally it is the males that have the most beautiful colours. All juveniles, however, are the same colour as the female and because of this can it be difficult to sex smaller fishes. For this reason you should obtain a small group and let them grow up together.

In the lake most species live in relatively shallow water on the rocky coast where the water is rich in oxygen, and because of this it is necessary to have powerful filtration (turnover at least 3 times the aquarium volume per hour) in Malawi cichlid aquaria.

Malawi cichlids should be fed with a food whose composition approximates as closely as possible to the natural food. Nowadays there are good flake foods and pellets (that do not contain animal fat) with a vegetable content. Most Malawi cichlids can also be offered small crustaceans such as mysis, *Cyclops*, and krill. On the other hand bloodworm is not a suitable food for Malawi cichlids. For additional information see the chapter about food in the first part of the book.

Name: *Aristochromis christyi*
Family: Cichlidae.
Range: Throughout Lake Malawi.
Temp: 23-27°C.   **Max.Size**: 30 cm.
Water: pH 7.5-8.5 **Aquarium**: 200 cm
Difficulty: 3
Comments: Carnivorous. Piscivorous. Eats all normal foods, incl. fishes up to 8-10 cm. Solitary. Mouth brooder. Territorial. Needs several hiding-places.

Name: *Aulonocara baenschi*
Family: Cichlidae.
Trade name: Benga Peacock.
Range: Lake Malawi: Nkhomo Reef.
Temp: 23-27°C.   **Max.Size**: 9 cm.
Water: pH 7.5-8.5 **Aquarium**: 110 cm
Difficulty: 3
Comments: Carnivorous. Frozen foods, but also dry foods. Mouth brooder. Territorial, but peaceful. Needs several hiding-places. Females are brownish. 9 cm is maximum size in the wild, but may grow larger in aquarium.

141

Name: *Aulonocara hueseri*
Family: Cichlidae.
Trade name: *A.* "white top" and "Night".
Range: Lake Malawi: Likoma Island.
Temp: 23-27°C.   **Max.Size**: 9 cm.
Water: pH 7.5-8.5 **Aquarium**: 110 cm
Difficulty: 3
Comments: Carnivorous. Frozen foods, but also dry foods. Mouth brooder. Territorial, but peaceful. Needs several hiding-places. Females are brownish. 9 cm is maximum size in the wild, but may grow larger in aquarium.

Name: *Aulonocara jacobfreibergi*
Family: Cichlidae.
Trade name: *Trematocranus jacob-freibergi*, T. trevori, T. carolae.
Range: Lake Malawi: Mostly in the rocky habitat.
Temp: 23-27°C.   **Max.Size**: 13 cm.
Water: pH 7.5-8.5 **Aquarium**: 120 cm
Difficulty: 3   **Comments**: Carnivorous. Frozen foods, but also dry foods. Mouth brooder. Territorial (inside a cave), but relatively peaceful. Needs several hiding-places. Females are brownish. Exists in several colour variants.

Name: *Aulonocara kandeense*
Family: Cichlidae.
Trade name: Aulocara Blue Orchid.
Range: Lake Malawi: Kande Island.
Temp: 23-27°C.   **Max.Size**: 12 cm.
Water: pH 7.5-8.5 **Aquarium**: 110 cm
Difficulty: 3
Comments: Carnivorous. Frozen foods, but also dry foods. Mouth brooder. Territorial, but relatively peaceful. Needs several hiding-places. Females are brownish.

Name: *Aulonocara stuartgranti*
Family: Cichlidae.
Trade name: *A. nyassae*, A. "Red flush", A. "Usisya", A. "Cobwe", A. "Maulana".
Range: Lake Malawi: Close to rocks.
Temp: 23-27°C.   **Max.Size**: 12 cm.
Water: pH 7.5-8.5 **Aquarium**: 110 cm
Difficulty: 3
Comments: Carnivorous. Frozen foods, but also dry foods. Mouth brooder. Territorial, but relatively peaceful. Needs several hiding-places. Females are brownish. Exists in several colour variants

Name: *Cheilochromis euchilus*
Family: Cichlidae.
Trade name: *Chilotilapia euchilus*.
Range: Lake Malawi: sandy areas.
Temp: 23-27°C.   **Max.Size**: 22 cm.
Water: pH 7.5-8.5 **Aquarium**: 160 cm
Difficulty: 3
Comments: Herbivorous and omnivorous. Eats all normal foods, but needs vegetable foods. Mouth brooder. Solitary. Territorial, but relatively peaceful. Needs several hiding-places. Females are silvery with black lines.

Name: *Copadichromis borleyi*
Family: Cichlidae.
Trade name: *Haplochromis borleyi*.
Range: Lake Malawi: throughout the lake.
Temp: 23-27°C.   **Max.Size**: 15 cm.
Water: pH 7.5-8.5 **Aquarium**: 150 cm
Difficulty: 3
Comments: Carnivorous. Frozen foods, but also dry foods. Mouth brooder. Territorial, but relatively peaceful. Needs several hiding-places. Females are silvery.

Name: *Copadichromis verduyni*
Family: Cichlidae.
Trade name: Haplochromis borleyi eastern.
Range: Between Eccles Reef and Gome.
Temp: 23-27°C.   **Max.Size**: 11 cm.
Water: pH 7.5-8.5 **Aquarium**: 120 cm
Difficulty: 3
Comments: Carnivorous. Frozen foods, but also dry foods. Mouth brooder. Territorial, and somewhat aggressive towards males of their own kind. Needs several hiding-places. Females are silvery.

Name: *Cynotilapia afra* "Cobue"
Family: Cichlidae.
Range: Lake Malawi: Rocky habitat, Cobwe.
Temp: 23-27°C.   **Max.Size**: 9 cm.
Water: pH 7.5-8.5 **Aquarium**: 110 cm
Difficulty: 3
Comments: Carnivorous. Frozen foods, but also dry foods. Mouth brooder. Territorial, and somewhat aggressive towards males of their own kind. Needs several hiding-places.

143

Name: *Cynotilapia* sp. "Lion".
Family: Cichlidae.
Range: Lake Malawi: Intermediate habitat.
Temp: 23-27°C.   **Max.Size**: 9 cm.
Water: pH 7.5-8.5 **Aquarium**: 110 cm
Difficulty: 3
Comments: Omnivorous. Frozen foods, but also dry foods. Mouth brooder. Territorial, and somewhat aggressive when breeding. Needs several hiding-places.

Name: *Cynotilapia* sp. "Mbamba".
Family: Cichlidae.
Range: Lake Malawi: Deep rocky biotope.
Temp: 23-27°C.   **Max.Size**: 10 cm.
Water: pH 7.5-8.5 **Aquarium**: 110 cm
Difficulty: 3
Comments: Omnivorous. Frozen foods, but also dry foods. Mouth brooder. Territorial, and somewhat aggressive when breeding. Needs several hiding-places.

Name: *Cyrtocara moorii*
Family: Cichlidae.
Trade name: *Haplochromis moorii*, Malawi Blue Dolphin.
Range: Lake Malawi, Lake Malombe.
Temp: 23-27°C.   **Max.Size**: 20 cm.
Water: pH 7.5-8.5 **Aquarium**: 150 cm
Difficulty: 3
Comments: Carnivorous. Frozen foods, but also dry foods. Mouth brooder. Peaceful. Needs several hiding-places. Fine sand as substrate. One of the most popular Malawi cichlids.

Name: *Dimidochromis compressiceps*
Family: Cichlidae.
Trade name: *Haplochromis compressiceps,* Malawi Eye-biter.
Range: Lake Malawi: shallow waters with Vallisneria beds.
Temp: 23-27°C.   **Max.Size**: 23 cm.
Water: pH 7.5-8.5 **Aquarium**: 160 cm
Difficulty: 4
Comments: Piscivorous. Eat small fishes, mainly juveniles. Frozen foods, but also dry foods. Mouth brooder. Territorial and aggressive when breeding.

Name: *Fossorochromis rostratus*
Family: Cichlidae.
Trade name: *Haplochromis rostratus*.
Range: Lake Malawi: sandy areas.
Temp: 23-27°C.   **Max.Size**: 30 cm.
Water: pH 7.5-8.5 **Aquarium**: 200 cm ·
Difficulty: 3
Comments: Carnivorous. Frozen foods, but also dry foods. Mouth brooder. Territorial and somewhat aggressive when breeding. Female silver-grey with black markings.

Name: *Iodotropheus sprengerae*
Family: Cichlidae.
Trade name: Rusty cichlid.
Range: Lake Malawi: rocky habitat.
Temp: 23-27°C.   **Max.Size**: 9 cm.
Water: pH 7.5-8.5 **Aquarium**: 100 cm
Difficulty: 2
Comments: Omnivorous. Eats all normal foods. Mouth brooder. Males are somewhat aggressive towards its own kind. Needs several hiding-places.

Name: *Labeotropheus fuelleborni*
Family: Cichlidae.
Range: Lake Malawi: upper rocky habitat.
Temp: 23-27°C.   **Max.Size**: 18 cm.
Water: pH 7.5-8.5 **Aquarium**: 120 cm
Difficulty: 3
Comments: Herbivorous. Eats all normal foods, but needs vegetable foods. Mouth brooder. Males are aggressive when breeding. Needs several hiding-places. Exists in several colour variants around the lake.

Name: *Labeotropheus trewavasae*
"Thumbi west"
Family: Cichlidae.
Range: Lake Malawi: rocky habitat.
Temp: 23-27°C.   **Max.Size**: 15 cm.
Water: pH 7.5-8.5 **Aquarium**: 120 cm
Difficulty: 3
Comments: Herbivorous. Eats all normal foods, but needs vegetable foods. Mouth brooder. Males are somewhat aggressive when breeding. Needs several hiding-places. Exists in several colour variants around the lake.

Name: *Labeotropheus trewavasae* "Lumbaulo"
Family: Cichlidae.
Range: Lake Malawi: rocky habitat.
Temp: 23-27°C.   **Max.Size**: 15 cm.
Water: pH 7.5-8.5 **Aquarium**: 120 cm
Difficulty: 3
Comments: See *L. trewavasae* "Thumbi West". *L. trewavasae* (and *L.fuelleborni*) females may occur in several colour variants on different places: brownish, orange, and OB (orange blotched).

Name: *Labidochromis caeruleus* "golden"
Family: Cichlidae.
Trade name: Yellow Labidochromis, Electric Yellow.
Range: L. Malawi: Charo to Lion's Cove
Temp: 23-27°C.   **Max.Size**: 10 cm.
Water: pH 7.5-8.5 **Aquarium**: 80 cm
Difficulty: 2
Comments: Carnivorous and omnivorous. Frozen foods, but also dry foods. Mouth brooder. Peaceful. Little territorial aggression. Needs several hiding-places. Popular aquarium fish.

Name: *Lethrinops* sp. "nyassae"
Family: Cichlidae.
Range: Lake Malawi: sandy areas.
Temp: 23-27°C.   **Max.Size**: 14 cm.
Water: pH 7.5-8.5 **Aquarium**: 100 cm
Difficulty: 3
Comments: Carnivorous. Frozen foods, but also dry foods. Mouth brooder. Peaceful. Little territorial aggression. Fine sand as substrate.

Name: *Melanochromis auratus* (female)
Family: Cichlidae.
Trade name: Nyassa golden cichlid.
Range: Lake Malawi: southern part.
Temp: 23-27°C.   **Max.Size**: 11 cm.
Water: pH 7.5-8.5 **Aquarium**: 110 cm
Difficulty: 3
Comments: Carnivorous and herbivorous. Eats all normal foods. Mouth brooder. Territorial. Males are aggressive towards its own kind. Males are black with pale yellow-white bands.

Name: *Melanochromis chipokae*
Family: Cichlidae.
Range: Lake Malawi: mainly Chidunga Rocks.
Temp: 23-27°C.   **Max.Size**: 14 cm.
Water: pH 7.5-8.5 **Aquarium**: 120 cm
Difficulty: 3
Comments: Carnivorous and piscivorous. Eats all normal foods, including small fishes. Mouth brooder. Territorial. Males are aggressive towards its own kind. Females are yellowish with black lines.

Name: *Melanochromis joanjohnsonae*
Family: Cichlidae.
Trade name: *Labidochromis joanjohnsonae*, Pearl of Likoma.
Range: Lake Malawi: Likoma Island.
Temp: 23-27°C.   **Max.Size**: 10 cm.
Water: pH 7.5-8.5 **Aquarium**: 80 cm
Difficulty: 2
Comments: Omnivorous. Frozen foods, but also dry foods with vegetable content. Mouth brooder. Peaceful. Females are silvery with reddish spots.

Name: *Nimbochromis livingstonii*
Family: Cichlidae.
Trade name: *Haplochromis livingstoni*, Kalingono.
Range: Lake Malawi: throughout the lake.
Temp: 23-27°C.   **Max.Size**: 25 cm.
Water: pH 7.5-8.5 **Aquarium**: 160 cm
Difficulty: 3
Comments: Carnivorous and piscivorous. Eats all normal foods, including small fishes. Mouth brooder. Somewhat aggressive. Males in breeding coloration are bluish.

Name: *Nimbochromis venustus*
Family: Cichlidae.
Trade name: *Haplochromis venustus*.
Range: Lake Malawi: sandy areas.
Temp: 23-27°C.   **Max.Size**: 23 cm.
Water: pH 7.5-8.5 **Aquarium**: 160 cm
Difficulty: 3
Comments: Carnivorous and piscivorous. Eats all normal foods, including small fishes. Mouth brooder. Somewhat aggressive.

Name: *Metriaclima aurora*
Family: Cichlidae.
Trade name: *Pseudotropheus aurora.*
Range: Lake Malawi: Likoma Island etc.
Temp: 23-27°C.   **Max.Size**: 11 cm.
Water: pH 7.5-8.5 **Aquarium**: 100 cm
Difficulty: 3
Comments: Omnivorous. Eats all normal foods, but needs vegetable foods. Mouth brooder. Territorial when breeding. Males dig tunnel-nests beneath rocks, in which spawning take place.

Name: *Metriaclima livingstonii*
Family: Cichlidae.
Trade name: *Pseudotropheus living-stonii, Ps. lanistocola.*
Range: Lake Malawi and Lake Malombe.
Temp: 23-27°C.   **Max.Size**: 14 cm.
Water: pH 7.5-8.5 **Aquarium**: 100 cm
Difficulty: 3   **Comments**: Omnivorous. Frozen foods, but also dry foods. Mouth brooder. Territorial when breeding. Non-breeding individuals occur over sandy areas with empty shells, breeds in the rocky habitat.

Name: *Metriaclima estherae* (male)
Family: Cichlidae.
Trade name: *Pseudotropheus estherae*, Red zebra.
Range: Lake Malawi: east coast.
Temp: 23-27°C.   **Max.Size**: 11 cm.
Water: pH 7.5-8.5 **Aquarium**: 120 cm
Difficulty: 3
Comments: Herbivorous and omnivorous. Eats all normal foods, but needs vegetable foods. Mouth brooder. Territorial when breeding. Males are normally blue, but orange also occur.

Name: *Metriaclima estherae* (female)
Family: Cichlidae.
Trade name: *Pseudotropheus estherae*, Red zebra.
Range: Lake Malawi: east coast.
Temp: 23-27°C.   **Max.Size**: 11 cm.
Water: pH 7.5-8.5 **Aquarium**: 120 cm
Difficulty: 3
Comments: Herbivorous. Eats all normal foods, but needs vegetable foods. Mouth brooder. Territorial when breeding. Females are normally orange-red, but OB (orange blotched) are also common.

Metriaclima callainos

Metriaclima greshakei

Metriaclima zebra Chilumba

Metriaclima fainzilberi

Metriaclima zebra gold

Metriaclima zebra

Name: *Metriaclima zebra*
Family: Cichlidae.
Trade name: *Pseudotropheus zebra*.
Range: Lake Malawi: rocky habitat.
Temp: 23-27°C.   **Max.Size**: 12-14 cm.
Water: pH 7.5-8.5   **Aquarium**: 120 cm
Difficulty: 3
Comments: Herbivorous and omnivorous (some carnivorous). Eats all normal foods, but needs vegetable foods. Mouth brooder. Territorial when breeding. Many different species/variants are currently labelled "zebra".

Metriaclima zebra

149

Name: *Otopharynx hetorodon*
Family: Cichlidae.
Trade name: *Haplochromis heterodon*.
Range: Lake Malawi: all rocky coasts.
Temp: 23-27°C.   **Max.Size**: 15 cm.
Water: pH 7.5-8.5 **Aquarium**: 120 cm
Difficulty: 3
Comments: Carnivorous. Frozen foods, but also dry foods. Mouth brooder. Territorial when breeding, but relatively peaceful. Sand as substrate.

Name: *Placidochromis milomo*
Family: Cichlidae.
Trade name: Haplochromis Super VC 10.
Range: Lake Malawi: deeper rocky habitat.
Temp: 23-27°C.   **Max.Size**: 25 cm.
Water: pH 7.5-8.5 **Aquarium**: 160 cm
Difficulty: 3
Comments: Carnivorous. Frozen foods, but also dry foods. Mouth brooder. Territorial when breeding, but relatively peaceful.

Name: *Protomelas taeniolatus*
Family: Cichlidae.
Trade name: Haplochromis steveni, H."Fire Blue" etc.
Range: Lake Malawi: rocky habitat.
Temp: 23-27°C.   **Max.Size**: 13-19 cm.
Water: pH 7.5-8.5 **Aquarium**: 150 cm
Difficulty: 3
Comments: Omnivorous. Frozen foods, but also dry foods with vegetable content. Mouth brooder. Territorial when breeding, but relatively peaceful. Many variants exist around the lake.

Name: *Pseudotropheus crabro*
Family: Cichlidae.
Trade name: Ps. chameleo.
Range: Lake Malawi: rocky habitat.
Temp: 23-27°C.   **Max.Size**: 12 cm.
Water: pH 7.5-8.5 **Aquarium**: 120 cm
Difficulty: 3
Comments: Carnivorous. Frozen foods, but also dry foods. Mouth brooder. Territorial when breeding, but relatively peaceful. In the lake this species cleans parasites from the catfish *Bagrus meridionalis*.

Name: *Pseudotropheus demasoni*
Family: Cichlidae.
Range: Lake Malawi: Ndumbi Point, Pombo Rocks.
Temp: 23-27°C.　**Max.Size**: 7 cm.
Water: pH 7.5-8.5　**Aquarium**: 110 cm
Difficulty: 3
Comments: Herbivorous and omnivorous. Frozen foods, but also dry foods with vegetable content. Mouth brooder. Peaceful with very little territorial behaviour.

Name: *Pseudotropheus saulosi* (female).
Family: Cichlidae.
Range: Lake Malawi: Taiwan Reef.
Temp: 23-27°C.　**Max.Size**: 7 cm.
Water: pH 7.5-8.5　**Aquarium**: 120 cm
Difficulty: 3
Comments: Herbivorous and omnivorous. Frozen foods, but also dry foods with vegetable content. Mouth brooder. Males (bluish with black bars) are rather territorial and aggressive towards males of its own kind.

Name: *Pseudotropheus socolofi*
Family: Cichlidae.
Trade name: Ps. pindani.
Range: Lake Malawi: central eastern shore.
Temp: 23-27°C.　**Max.Size**: 7 cm.
Water: pH 7.5-8.5　**Aquarium**: 80 cm
Difficulty: 2
Comments: Carnivorous and omnivorous. Frozen foods, but also dry foods with vegetable content. Mouth brooder. Peaceful with very little territorial behaviour.

Name: *Sciaenochromis fryeri*
Family: Cichlidae.
Trade name: *Haplochromis ahli*, Electric blue.
Range: Lake Malawi: throughout the lake.
Temp: 23-27°C.　**Max.Size**: 16 cm.
Water: pH 7.5-8.5　**Aquarium**: 120 cm
Difficulty: 3
Comments: Carnivorous. Piscivorous, feeding mainly on small mbuna. Frozen foods, but also dry foods. Mouth brooder. Very little territorial behaviour. Females are brownish.

151

Tanganyika Cichlids

Lake Tanganyika is the sixth largest lake in the world and lies in east Africa. It is extremely deep — 1470 metres. As far as hobbyists are concerned the rocky coasts are the most interesting parts, since it is here that are found most of the species (mainly cichlids, but also some catfishes) that are kept in aquaria. More than 200 different cichlid species have been exported for the aquarium hobby, and today most of them are being bred. As in Lake Malawi, most of the cichlids of Lake Tanganyika are endemic (exist in just one location).

The water in Lake Tanganyika is alkaline (pH 8.6-9.2) and because of this the aquarium water must have a pH of at least 7.5, ideally 8.0. The water temperature in the aquarium should be between 24 and 26° C. The water in the lake is very clear and the top 40 metres is rich in oxygen. The oxygen content in the aquarium water is therefore very important. This means that you must be strict about the changing of water (app. 30% each week) and have powerful filtration (turnover at least 3 times the aquarium volume per hour).

There are only a few species of plants in the lake but it is possible to have aquatic plants such as *Vallisneria, Anubias, Crinum*, and *Ceratophyllum* with Tanganyika cichlids. It is much more common to decorate a Tanganyika aquarium with rocks and/or a rocky background.

In Lake Tanganyika there are both mouthbrooding and substrate brooding cichlids (see BREEDING). The mouthbrooding species should be kept in large aquaria (at least 150 cm long) with a relatively large number of each kind (app. 10-15) and it is also better with more males than females. Some of the substrate-brooding species can be kept either as pairs or in small groups in relatively small aquaria (from 60 l upwards). There can, however, be problems in sexing and because of this is it better to buy a small group (4-6) of young fishes and let them grow up together.

Most of the Tanganyika cichlids will eat what they are offered in the aquarium (even if their digestive system is not adjusted to that kind of food). Hence they should be fed using a food whose composition as closely as possible resembles their natural food. Nowadays there are good flake and granulate foods (that do not contain animal fat) with a vegetable content. Most Tanganyika cichlids can also be offered small crustaceans such as mysis, Cyclops and krill. On the other hand bloodworm is not a suitable food for Tanganyika cichlids. For additional information see the chapter about food in the first part of this book.

Name: *Altolamprologus compressiceps*
Family: Cichlidae
Trade name: *Lamprologus compressiceps.*
Range: Lake Tanganyika: rocky coast.
Temp: 23-26°C   **Max.Size**: 16 cm.
Water: pH 7.8-9   **Aquarium**: 100 cm.
Difficulty: 3
Comments: Carnivorous. Eats all normal foods. Pairing fish. Territorial. Substrate (cave) brooder. Breeds in empty snail shells, big enough for the female. Needs hiding-places. Exists in several colour variants.

Name: *Chalinochromis brichardi*
Family: Cichlidae
Range: Lake Tanganyika: rocky coast.
Temp: 23-26°C   **Max.Size**: 16 cm.
Water: pH 7.8-9   **Aquarium**: 100 cm.
Difficulty: 2
Comments: Carnivorous. Eats all normal foods. Pairing fish. Territorial. Substrate (cave) brooder. Needs hiding-places. Start with a small group and let these pair off.

Name: *Cyathopharynx foae*
Family: Cichlidae
Trade name: *Cyathopharynx furcifer.*
Range: Lake Tanganyika: rocky coast.
Temp: 23-26°C   **Max.Size**: 22 cm.
Water: pH 7.8-9   **Aquarium**: 200 cm.
Difficulty: 4
Comments: Carnivorous and omnivorous. Eats all normal foods, but prefers frozen foods. Territorial. Mouthbrooder. Needs hiding-places. Start with a group tank raised specimens. Exists in several colour variants.

153

Name: *Cyphotilapia frontosa*
Family: Cichlidae
Trade name: Tanganyika humphead.
Range: Lake Tanganyika: rocky coast.
Temp: 23-26°C   **Max.Size**: 40 cm.
Water: pH 7.8-9   **Aquarium**: 200 cm.
Difficulty: 3
Comments: Carnivorous. Eats all normal foods, including fishes. Peaceful, but eats smaller tankmates. Mouthbrooder. Needs hiding-places. Best kept in a group with 5-6 specimens. Exists in several geographical variants.

Name: *Cyprichromis leptosoma*
Family: Cichlidae
Range: Lake Tanganyika.
Temp: 23-26°C   **Max.Size**: 8 cm.
Water: pH 7.8-9   **Aquarium**: 150 cm.
Difficulty: 3
Comments: Carnivorous. Frozen and live foods, but also dry foods. Mouthbrooder. Best kept in a group with 10 or more. Males are aggressive towards their own kind. Exists in several colour variants.

Name: *Enantiopus melanogenys*
Family: Cichlidae
Range: Lake Tanganyika: sandy range.
Temp: 23-26°C   **Max.Size**: 15 cm.
Water: pH 7.8-9   **Aquarium**: 150 cm.
Difficulty: 3
Comments: Carnivorous. Frozen and live foods, but also dry foods. Mouthbrooder. Best kept in a group with 10 or more. Males are aggressive towards their own kind. Needs fine sand.

Name: *Eretmodus cyanostictus*
Family: Cichlidae
Trade name: Goby cichlid.
Range: Lake Tanganyika: shallow water.
Temp: 23-26°C   **Max.Size**: 8 cm.
Water: pH 7.8-9   **Aquarium**: 120 cm.
Difficulty: 3
Comments: Carnivorous and herbivorous. Eats all normal foods. Mouthbrooder (both male and female brood the eggs). Best kept in a small group with 6 or more. Males are territorial. Needs hiding-places and oxygen-rich water.

Name: *Julidochromis dickfeldi*
Family: Cichlidae
Trade name: Dickfeld's Julie.
Range: Lake Tanganyika: southwestern part.
Temp: 23-26°C **Max.Size**: 10 cm.
Water: pH 7.8-9 **Aquarium**: 60 cm.
Difficulty: 3
Comments: Carnivorous. Eats all normal foods. Substrate (cave) brooder. Pairing fish. Needs hiding-places. Start with a small group and let them pair off. Territorial.

Name: *Julidochromis marlieri*
Family: Cichlidae
Trade name: Marlier's Julie.
Range: Lake Tanganyika: rocky coast.
Temp: 23-26°C **Max.Size**: 13 cm.
Water: pH 7.8-9 **Aquarium**: 80 cm.
Difficulty: 3
Comments: Carnivorous. Eats all normal foods. Substrate (cave) brooder. Pairing fish. Needs hiding-places. Start with a small group and let them pair off. Territorial.

Name: *Julidochromis ornatus*
Family: Cichlidae
Range: Lake Tanganyika: rocky coast.
Temp: 23-26°C **Max.Size**: 9 cm.
Water: pH 7.8-9 **Aquarium**: 60 cm.
Difficulty: 3
Comments: Carnivorous. Eats all normal foods. Substrate (cave) brooder. Pairing fish. Needs hiding-places. Start with a small group and let them pair off. Territorial. Not together with *J. transcriptus.*

Name: *Julidochromis regani*
Family: Cichlidae
Range: Lake Tanganyika.
Temp: 23-26°C **Max.Size**: 13 cm.
Water: pH 7.8-9 **Aquarium**: 70 cm.
Difficulty: 3
Comments: Carnivorous. Eats all normal foods. Substrate (cave) brooder. Pairing fish. Needs hiding-places. Start with a small group and let them pair off. Territorial.

Name: *Julidochromis transcriptus*
Family: Cichlidae
Trade name: Julidochromis kissi.
Range: Northwestern Lake Tanganyika.
Temp: 23-26°C   **Max.Size**: 7 cm.
Water: pH 7.8-9   **Aquarium**: 50 cm.
Difficulty: 3
Comments: Carnivorous. Eats all normal foods. Substrate (cave) brooder. Pairing fish. Needs hiding-places. Start with a small group and let them pair off. Territorial. Not together with *J. ornatus.*

Name: *Lamprologus ocellatus*
Family: Cichlidae
Trade name: Golden/Red ocellatus.
Range: Lake Tanganyika.
Temp: 23-26°C   **Max.Size**: 6 cm.
Water: pH 7.8-9   **Aquarium**: 50 cm.
Difficulty: 3
Comments: Carnivorous. Eats all normal foods. Substrate brooder. Breeds in empty snails. Best kept in a small group with 6 or more. Needs fine sand. Rather peaceful.

Name: *Neolamprologus brichardi.*
Family: Cichlidae
Trade name: Princess of Burundi.
Range: Throughout Lake Tanganyika.
Temp: 23-26°C   **Max.Size**: 10 cm.
Water: pH 7.8-9   **Aquarium**: 80 cm.
Difficulty: 2
Comments: Carnivorous. Eats all normal foods. Substrate (cave) brooder. Pairing fish. Needs several hiding-places (caves). Best kept in a small group with 6 or more. Juveniles up to 2.5 cm help guard younger siblings. Territorial.

Name: *Neolamprologus leleupi*
Family: Cichlidae
Trade name: *Lamprologus longior.*
Range: Throughout Lake Tanganyika.
Temp: 23-26°C   **Max.Size**: 11 cm.
Water: pH 7.8-9   **Aquarium**: 100 cm.
Difficulty: 4
Comments: Carnivorous. Eats all normal foods. Substrate (cave) brooder. Needs several hiding-places. Start with a small group and let them pair off. Territorial and very aggressive towards its own kind.

Name: *Neolamprologus multifasciatus.*
Family: Cichlidae
Range: Lake Tanganyika: Zambian waters.
Temp: 23-26°C **Max.Size**: 4 cm.
Water: pH 7.8-9 **Aquarium**: 60 cm.
Difficulty: 2
Comments: Carnivorous. Eats all normal foods. Substrate brooder. Breeds in empty snails. Best kept in a small group with 8 or more. Needs fine sand. Digs a lot.

Name: *Ophthalmotilapia ventralis*
Family: Cichlidae
Range: Lake Tanganyika: Rocky coast.
Temp: 23-26°C **Max.Size**: 4 cm.
Water: pH 7.8-9 **Aquarium**: 160 cm.
Difficulty: 3
Comments: Herbivorous and carnivorous. Live and frozen foods, but also dry foods. Mouthbrooder. Territorial. Rather aggressive towards its own kind. Needs fine sand.

Name: *Petrochromis trewavasae*
Family: Cichlidae
Range: Lake Tanganyika: rocky coast.
Temp: 23-26°C **Max.Size**: 17 cm.
Water: pH 7.8-9 **Aquarium**: 200 cm.
Difficulty: 4
Comments: Herbivorous. Vegetable-based foods necessary. Mouthbrooder. Needs several hiding-places. Territorial. Very aggressive towards its own kind. Max. 1 male per aquarium.

Name: *Spathodus erythrodon*
Family: Cichlidae
Trade name: Goby cichlid.
Range: Lake Tanganyika: shallow water.
Temp: 23-26°C **Max.Size**: 8 cm.
Water: pH 7.8-9 **Aquarium**: 100 cm.
Difficulty: 3
Comments: Omnivorous. Eats all normal foods. Mouthbrooder (both male and female brood the eggs). Best kept in a small group with 6 or more. Males are territorial. Needs hiding-places and oxygen-rich water.

157

Name: *Tanganicodus irsacae*
Family: Cichlidae
Trade name: Goby cichlid.
Range: Lake Tanganyika: shallow water.
Temp: 23-26°C   **Max.Size**: 6,5 cm.
Water: pH 7.8-9   **Aquarium**: 100 cm.
Difficulty: 3
Comments: Carnivorous and herbivorous. Eats all normal foods. Mouthbrooder (both male and female brood the eggs). Best kept in a small group with 6 or more. Males are territorial. Needs hiding-places and oxygen-rich water.

Name: *Tropheus annectens*
Family: Cichlidae
Trade name: *Tropheus polli.*
Range: Lake Tanganyika: upper rocky habitat.
Temp: 23-26°C   **Max.Size**: 14 cm.
Water: pH 7.8-9   **Aquarium**: 160 cm.
Difficulty: 3
Comments: Herbivorous. Vegetable-based foods necessary. Mouthbrooder. Best kept in a group with 10 or more. Territorial. Needs several hiding-places.

Name: *Tropheus brichardi* Kavala
Family: Cichlidae
Range: Lake Tanganyika: upper rocky habitat.
Temp: 23-26°C   **Max.Size**: 13 cm.
Water: pH 7.8-9   **Aquarium**: 200 cm.
Difficulty: 3
Comments: Herbivorous. Vegetable-based foods necessary. Mouthbrooder. Best kept in a group with 10 or more. Territorial. Needs several hiding-places. Exists in several colour variants. See also next page, bottom right.

Name: *Tropheus duboisi*
Family: Cichlidae
Range: Lake Tanganyika: upper rocky habitat.
Temp: 23-26°C   **Max.Size**: 13 cm.
Water: pH 7.8-9   **Aquarium**: 160 cm.
Difficulty: 3
Comments: Herbivorous. Vegetable-based foods necessary. Mouthbrooder. Best kept in a group with 8 or more. Territorial. Needs several hiding-places. Juveniles are spotted, adults have a stripe. See next page, bottom left.

Tropheus sp. "black" Kiriza

Tropheus sp. "black" Kirschfleck

Tropheus sp. "black" Magara

Tropheus sp. "black" Pemba

Tropheus sp. "ikola"

Name: *Tropheus* sp. "black"
Family: Cichlidae
Range: Tanganyika: upper rocky habitat.
Temp: 23-26°C   **Max.Size:** 13 cm.
Water: pH 7.8-9   **Aquarium**: 200 cm.
Difficulty: 3
Comments: Herbivorous. Vegetable-based foods necessary. Mouthbrooder. Best kept in a group with 10 or more. Territorial. Needs several hiding-places. Exists in many colour variants throughout the lake, some are shown here.

Tropheus duboisi Maswa

Tropheus brichardi Ulwile

159

Tropheus moorii Chaitika

Tropheus moorii Mpulungu

Tropheus moorii Kasanga

Tropheus moorii Lufubu

Tropheus moorii Murago

Tropheus sp. "red" Chimba

Name: *Tropheus* sp. "red" and *Tropheus moorii*.
Family: Cichlidae
Range: Tanganyika: upper rocky habitat.
Temp: 23-26°C   **Max.Size**: 14 cm.
Water: pH 7.8-9   **Aquarium**: 200 cm.
Difficulty: 3   **Comments**: Herbivorous. Vegetable-based foods necessary. Mouthbrooder. Best kept in a group with 10 or more. Territorial. Needs several hiding-places. *T.* sp "red" and *T. moorii* exist in many colour variants throughout the lake, some are shown here.

Tropheus sp. "red" Kachese

160

Other Cichlids

Cichlids are found over almost the entire African continent. A number of the cichlids that are seen in the trade come from West Africa, where they live in rivers, streams, and pools. The water in these areas varies a lot, but is relatively soft and the pH is normally between 6.5-7.5, with a temperature around 24-26°C.

The water in the great lakes (Victoria, Tanganyika, and Malawi) is alkaline and the pH varies seasonally between 7 and 9, the temperature between 23 and 29°C. The rivers of Madagascar contain relatively soft water.

You should feed these fishes with a food which is as similar as possible in composition to their natural food. Nowadays there are good flake foods and pellets (that do not contain animal fat) with a vegetable content. For additional information see the chapter on FOOD in the first section of this book.

It should be self-evident that there is a lot of variability among these cichlids given that such a large area with very variable conditions is involved. The rheophilic (from very fast-flowing water, e.g. rapids) cichlids, for example, have an atrophied swim-bladder that provides only minimal buoyancy, permitting them to remain on the bottom. In the areas where cichlids occur there are also many other fishes (e.g. tetras and catfishes), and these can often readily be mixed in the aquarium.

Victoria cichlids should never be kept in pairs, but instead in groups and in relatively large aquaria (at least 150 l). All these cichlids are mouthbrooders (see BREEDING). Suitable pH/temperature conditions in the aquarium are 7-8 and 24-26°C, respectively, even though these fishes are relatively adaptable.

Name: *Anomalochromis thomasi*
Family: Cichlidae
Trade name: African butterfly cichlid.
Habitat: Sierra Leone, Guinea, Liberia.
Temp: 24-26°C   **Max.Size**: 8 cm
Water: pH 6.0-7.5 **Aquarium**: 80 cm.
Difficulty: 1
Comments: Omnivorous. Eats all normal foods. Open substrate brooder. Pairing fish. Somewhat territorial. Peaceful. Needs hiding-places.

Name: *Astatotilapia latifasciata*
Family: Cichlidae
Trade name: *Haplochromis* "zebra obliquidens".
Habitat: Lake Kioga basin.
Temp: 23-26°C   **Max.Size**: 12 cm
Water: pH 7.0-8.0   **Aquarium**: 100 cm
Difficulty: 2
Comments: Omnivorous. Eats all normal foods. The male is territorial and aggressive. Mouthbrooder. Needs several hiding-places.

Name: *Astatotilapia nubila*
Family: Cichlidae
Trade name: *Haplochromis nubilus*
Habitat: Lake Victoria, Nabugado etc..
Temp: 23-26°C   **Max.Size**: 15 cm
Water: pH 7.0-8.0 **Aquarium**: 100 cm
Difficulty: 2
Comments: Carnivorous. Eats all normal foods. Somewhat territorial and aggressive. Mouthbrooder. Needs several hiding-places. Prolific and precocious breeder.

Name: *Chromidotilapia guntheri*
Family: Cichlidae
Trade name: Günther's mouthbrooder.
Habitat: Sierra Leone to Cameroon, Gabon.
Temp: 24-26°C   **Max.Size**: 18 cm
Water: 6.0-7.5   **Aquarium**: 100 cm.
Difficulty: 3
Comments: Omnivorous. Eats all normal foods. Pairing fish. Mouthbrooder. When breeding territorial and aggressive towards its own kind. Needs hiding-places.

Name: *Etroplus maculatus*
Family: Cichlidae
Trade name: Orange chromid.
Habitat: India, Sri Lanka.
Temp: 24-27°C   **Max.Size**: 10 cm
Water: pH 7.5-8.5 **Aquarium**: 70 cm
Difficulty: 3
Comments: Omnivorous. Eats all normal foods, also small fish fry. Open spawner. Pairing fish. Peaceful. Accepts freshwater, but prefer brackish. This is one of the very few Asian cichlids.

Name: *Haplochromis* sp. "Flameback"
Family: Cichlidae
Habitat: Lake Victoria.
Temp: 23-26°C   **Max.Size**: 10 cm
Water: pH 7.0-8.0 **Aquarium**: 110 cm
Difficulty: 2
Comments: Omnivorous. Eats all normal foods. The male is territorial and aggressive. Mouthbrooder. Needs several hiding-places. Females are silver-grey. Jumps.

Name: *Haplochromis nyererei*
Family: Cichlidae
Habitat: Lake Victoria.
Temp: 23-26°C   **Max.Size**: 12 cm
Water: pH 7.0-8.0 **Aquarium**: 120 cm
Difficulty: 2
Comments: Carnivorous. Eats all normal foods. The male is territorial and aggressive. Mouthbrooder. Needs several hiding-places. Female brownish.

Name: *Hemichromus lifalili*
Family: Cichlidae
Trade name: Blood-red jewel cichlid.
Habitat: West Africa.
Temp: 23-25°C   **Max.Size**: 11 cm
Water: 6.5-7.5   **Aquarium**: 100 cm.
Difficulty: 3
Comments: Omnivorous. Eats all normal foods. Pairing fish. Open substrate brooder. When breeding extremely territorial and aggressive. Needs hiding-places.

Name: *Lamprologus congoensis*
Family: Cichlidae
Trade name: Congo lamprologus.
Habitat: Rapids in lower Congo basin.
Temp: 23-26°C   **Max.Size**: 11 cm
Water: 6.5-7.5   **Aquarium**: 90 cm.
Difficulty: 3
Comments: Omnivorous. Eats all normal foods. Pair-forming or harem-breeding fish. Substrate (cave) brooder. Territorial towards its own kind. Reduced swim-bladder. Needs hiding-places. Jumps. Needs high oxygen levels.

Ad Konings

Name: *Nanochromis nudiceps*
Family: Cichlidae
Trade name: Nudiceps.
Habitat: Lower Congo basin.
Temp: 23-26°C   **Max.Size**: 9 cm
Water: 6.0-7.0   **Aquarium**: 120 cm.
Difficulty: 3
Comments: Omnivorous. Needs live and frozen foods. Pairing fish. Substrate (cave) brooder. Somewhat territorial towards its own kind. Needs hiding-places.

Name: *Paratilapia polleni*
Family: Cichlidae
Trade name: Marakely
Habitat: Madagascar.
Temp: 23-27°C   **Max.Size**: 30 cm
Water: pH 6.5-8.0 **Aquarium**: 200 cm
Difficulty: 4
Comments: Omnivorous. Eats all normal foods. Open substrate brooder. Males are aggressive towards their own kind. Only for large aquaria.

Name: *Pelvicachromis pulcher*
Family: Cichlidae
Trade name: Krib, Kribensis.
Habitat: Nigeria, Cameroon.
Temp: 23-26°C   **Max.Size**: 11 cm
Water: 6.0-7.5   **Aquarium**: 60 cm.
Difficulty: 2
Comments: Omnivorous. Eats all normal foods. Somewhat territorial when breeding. Pairing fish. Substrate (cave) brooder. Needs hiding-places. Good beginner's cichlid.

Name: *Pelvicachromis subocellatus*
Family: Cichlidae
Habitat: Gabon to mouth of Congo river.
Temp: 23-26°C   **Max.Size**: 9 cm
Water: 6.0-7.5   **Aquarium**: 80 cm.
Difficulty: 3
Comments: Omnivorous. Live and frozen foods, some flake foods. Territorial when breeding. Pairing fish. Substrate (cave) brooder. Needs hiding-places.

Name: *Pelvicachromis taeniatus* "red"
Family: Cichlidae
Habitat: Nigeria, Cameroon.
Temp: 23-26°C   **Max.Size**: 9 cm
Water: 6.0-7.0   **Aquarium**: 80 cm.
Difficulty: 3
Comments: Omnivorous. Live and frozen foods, some dry foods. Territorial when breeding. Pairing fish. Substrate (cave) brooder. Needs hiding-places. *P. taeniatus* exist in several geographical variants.

Name: *Pelvicachromis taeniatus*, female.
Family: Cichlidae
Trade name: Kumba Funge taeniatus.
Habitat: Cameroon: Kumba Funge.
Temp: 23-26°C   **Max.Size**: 9 cm
Water: 6.0-7.0   **Aquarium**: 80 cm.
Difficulty: 3
Comments: Omnivorous. Live and frozen foods, some dry foods. Territorial when breeding. Pairing fish. Substrate (cave) brooder. Needs hiding-places. *P. taeniatus* exist in several geographical variants.

Name: *Pseudocrenilabrus philander*
Family: Cichlidae
Habitat: Africa.
Temp: 22-25°C   **Max.Size**: 10 cm
Water: 6.5-7.5   **Aquarium**: 90 cm.
Difficulty: 3
Comments: Omnivorous. Eats all normal foods. Territorial. Somewhat aggressive when breeding. Mouthbrooder. Needs hiding-places.

Name: *Steatocranus casuarius*
Family: Cichlidae
Trade name: Lumphead, Blockhead.
Habitat: Rapids of lower Congo river, Malebo Pool.
Temp: 23-26°C   **Max.Size**: 13 cm
Water: 6.5-7.5   **Aquarium**: 90 cm.
Difficulty: 2
Comments: Omnivorous. Eats all normal foods. Pairing fish. Territorial. Somewhat aggressive when breeding. Substrate (cave) brooder. Reduced swimbladder. Needs hiding-places. Jumps.

Name: *Teleogramma brichardi*
Family: Cichlidae
Trade name: Brichard's teleo.
Habitat: Rapids of lower Congo river, Malebo Pool.
Temp: 23-26°C   **Max.Size**: 12 cm
Water: 6.5-7.5   **Aquarium**: 90 cm.
Difficulty: 3
Comments: Carnivorous. Eats all normal foods. Territorial: Very aggressive when breeding. Substrate (cave) brooder. Reduced swimbladder. Needs hiding-places. Jumps.

Name: *Tilapia buttikoferi*
Family: Cichlidae
Trade name: Zebra tilapia.
Habitat: Guinea-Bissau to west Liberia.
Temp: 22-25°C   **Max.Size**: 30 cm
Water: 6.0-7.0   **Aquarium**: 150 cm.
Difficulty: 3
Comments: Omnivorous. Eats all normal foods. Fully-grown fishes are piscivorous. Can eat plants. Open spawner. Very territorial and aggressive. Needs hiding-places.

Name: *Tilapia joka*
Family: Cichlidae
Habitat: Sierra Leone, Liberia.
Temp: 22-25°C   **Max.Size**: 20 cm
Water: 6.5-7.5   **Aquarium**: 100 cm.
Difficulty: 3
Comments: Omnivorous, largely herbivorous. Vegetable foods, but eats all normal foods. Good tuft-algae eater. Substrate (cave) brooder. Territorial, but relative peaceful. Needs hiding-places.

Name: *Tilapia mariae*
Family: Cichlidae
Trade name: Mariae, Mary's cichlid.
Habitat: Ivory Coast to Cameroon.
Temp: 22-25°C   **Max.Size**: 30 cm
Water: 6.0-7.5   **Aquarium**: 150 cm.
Difficulty: 3
Comments: Omnivorous, largely herbivorous. Eats plants, but also dry foods. Pairing fish. Substrate brooder. Territorial and aggressive. Digs a lot. Needs hiding-places.

Other Fishes

There are a number of aquarium fishes that cannot easily be assigned to any particular group, and to try would be pointless in a non-specialist book like this. Hence I have purposely left a number of fishes out of this categorisation. This "group" includes fishes different as the giant arowanas (*Osteoglossum*), several brackish-water fishes, the sterlet (*Acipenser ruthenus*), and so on. These fishes, of course, are very diverse and have very little in common as regards their living conditions, and hence the reader should refer to the text for each fish, plus the general text in the first part of the book.

Name: *Acipenser ruthenus*
Family: Acinpenseridae.
Trade name: Sterlet.
Range: Europe, Siberia.
Temp: 10-20°C.   **Max.Size**: 125 cm.
Water: pH 7-8   **Aquarium**: 500 cm.
Difficulty: 5
Comments: Carnivorous. Live and frozen foods. Peaceful. Not possible to breed in an aquarium. Too big for the aquarium and it is also a cold water fish. Better in ponds. Accepts brackish water.

Name: *Aethiomastacembelus ellipsifer*
Family: Mastacembelidae.
Trade name: Tanganyika eel.
Range: Lake Tanganyika.
Temp: 23-26°C.   **Max.Size**: 45 cm.
Water: pH 7.5-9.   **Aquarium**: 150 cm.
Difficulty: 3.
Comments: Carnivorous (piscivorous). Eats small fishes. Live foods. Solitary. Crepuscular and nocturnal. Sensitive. Needs fine sand and several hiding-places.

Mark Smith

Mark Smith

Name: *Allenbatrachus grunniens*
Family: Batrachoididae
Trade name: *Batrachus grunniens*,
Toadfish, frogfish.
Range: Indo-West Pacific.
Temp: 23-27°C.　　**Max.Size**: 30 cm.
Water: pH 7.5-8.5　**Aquarium**: 130 cm.
Difficulty: 5
Comments: Piscivorous. Eats small
fishes. Needs live foods. Bottom-oriented.
Needs brackish water (2-3%). Can make
quaking sounds.

Name: *Apteronotus albifrons*
Family: Apteronotidae.
Trade name: Black ghost.
Range: South America.
Temp: 22-27°C.　　**Max.Size**: 50 cm.
Water: pH 6-7.5　　**Aquarium**: 150 cm.
Difficulty: 4
Comments: Carnivorous. Live foods.
Nocturnal. Shy. Very aggressive towards
its own kind. Needs several hiding-places.
Dense planting. Sensitive.

Mark Smith

Mark Smith

Name: *Badis badis*
Family: Nandidae
Trade name: Chameleon fish.
Range: Southeast Asia.
Temp: 23-26°C.　　**Max.Size**: 8 cm.
Water: pH 6-7.5　　**Aquarium**: 100 cm.
Difficulty: 3
Comments: Carnivorous. Live or frozen
foods. Substrate (cave) brooder. Some-
what territorial towards its own kind.
Needs several hiding places and a sandy
substrate. Can quickly change its colour.

Name: *Campylomormyrus elephas*
Family: Mormyridae
Trade name: Blunt-jawed elephant nose.
Range: Congo basin.
Temp: 25-28°C.　　**Max.Size**: 40 cm.
Water: pH 6.5-7.5　**Aquarium**: 150 cm.
Difficulty: 4
Comments: Carnivorous. Live foods. Cre-
puscular and nocturnal. Fine sand (max.
2 mm) in aquarium. Very good water qual-
ity. Planted aquaria with an open swim-
ming area. Needs several hiding-places.

Name: *Channa asiatica*
Family: Channidae.
Trade name: Small snakehead.
Range: Japan, Taiwan, China, Sri Lanka.
Temp: 22-28°C.　　**Max.Size**: 25 cm.
Water: pH 6.5-7.5　**Aquarium**: 150 cm.
Difficulty: 3
Comments: Carnivorous (piscivorous). Keep only with large fishes. Live and frozen foods. Substrate (floating nest) brooder. Aggressive towards its own kind. Solitary. Intolerant of salt in the water.

Name: *Channa micropeltes*
Family: Channidae.
Trade name: Giant snakehead.
Range: Southeast Asia.
Temp: 24-28°C.　　**Max.Size**: 100 cm.
Water: pH 6.5-7.5　**Aquarium**: 400 cm.
Difficulty: 5
Comments: Piscivorous. Keep only with large fishes. Live and frozen foods. Substrate brooder. Aggressive towards its own kind. Solitary. Intolerant of salt in the water. Too big for the aquarium.

Name: *Coius quadrifasciatus*
Family: Coiidae.
Trade name: Four-barred tigerfish.
Range: Asia and Oceania.
Temp: 22-26°C.　　**Max.Size**: 35 cm.
Water: pH 6.5-7.5　**Aquarium**: 200 cm.
Difficulty: 4
Comments: Carnivorous (piscivorous). Keep only with large fishes. Eats live fishes and meat. Prefers brackish water. Needs dense planting (salt-tolerant plants) and several hiding-places.

Name: *Ctenogobius duospilus*
Family: Gobiidae.
Trade name: *Rhinogobius wui.*
Range: Eastern Asia.
Temp: 15-25°C.　　**Max.Size**: 4.5 cm.
Water: pH 6.5-7.5.　**Aquarium**: 60 cm.
Difficulty: 3.
Comments: Carnivorous. Needs small live and frozen foods. Substrate (cave) brooder. Air breather. Territorial at spawning time. Needs fine sand, several hiding-places (stones) and a strong current in the water.

Name: *Dormitator maculatus*
Family: Eleotridae.
Trade name: Sleeper goby.
Range: North Carolina (USA) to south-eastern Brazil.
Temp: 22-28°C.   **Max.Size**: 50 cm.
Water: pH 6.5-8   **Aquarium**: 250 cm.
Difficulty: 4
Comments: Carnivorous (piscivorous). Eats small fishes. Live and frozen foods. Needs brackish water. Somewhat territorial. Needs fine sand and several hiding-places. Too big for most aquaria.

Name: *Eigenmannia virescens*
Family: Sternopygidae.
Trade name: Glass knifefish.
Range: South America.
Temp: 22-28°C.   **Max.Size**: 45 cm.
Water: pH 6-7   **Aquarium**: 120 cm.
Difficulty: 4
Comments: Carnivorous. Live and frozen foods. Substrate (floating plants) spawner. Nocturnal. Shy. Needs floating plants and several hiding-places.

Name: *Erpetoichthys calabaricus*
Family: Polypteridae.
Trade name: Snakefish, reedfish.
Range: West Africa.
Temp: 23-28°C.   **Max.Size**: 70 cm.
Water: pH 6-7.5   **Aquarium**: 200 cm.
Difficulty: 4
Comments: Carnivorous (piscivorous). Eats small fishes. Live and frozen foods. Crepuscular and nocturnal. Shy. Peaceful. Needs fine sand, dense planting, and hiding-places. Jumps.

Name: *Gnathonemus petersii*
Family: Mormyridae.
Trade name: Elephantnose, Peters elephantnose.
Range: West Africa.
Temp: 23-28°C.   **Max.Size**: 35 cm.
Water: pH 6-7.5   **Aquarium**: 150 cm.
Difficulty: 3
Comments: Omnivorous. Eats all normal foods, but prefers live and frozen foods. Crepuscular and nocturnal. Shy. Peaceful, but aggressive towards its own kind. Territorial. Needs hiding-places. Jumps.

Name: *Gobioides broussoneti*
Family: Gobiidae.
Trade name: Violet goby.
Range: South Carolina (USA) to Brazil.
Temp: 23-26°C.   **Max.Size**: 55 cm.
Water: pH 6-7   **Aquarium**: 200 cm.
Difficulty: 5
Comments: Carnivorous. Live foods. Nocturnal. Shy. Peaceful, but very aggressive towards its own kind. Solitary. Territorial. Needs fine sand and hiding-places. Brackish water (1%).

Name: *Gymnarchus niloticus*
Family: Gymnarchidae.
Trade name: Nile pike.
Range: Nile, Niger, Gambia basin etc.
Temp: 23-26°C.   **Max.Size**: 170 cm.
Water: pH 6.5-7.5   **Aquarium**: 300 cm.
Difficulty: 5
Comments: Carnivorous. Piscivorous. Eats fishes and all normal foods. Crepuscular and nocturnal. Shy. Not an aquarium fish.

Name: *Hypogymnogobius xanthozona*
Family: Gobiidae.
Trade name: Bumblebee goby.
Range: Java, Sumatra, Borneo.
Temp: 25-28°C.   **Max.Size**: 4.5 cm.
Water: pH 6-7.   **Aquarium**: 60 cm.
Difficulty: 3
Comments: Carnivorous. Live and maybe frozen foods. Substrate (cave) brooder. Peaceful, but territorial towards its own kind. Needs several hiding-places and fine dark sand. Brackish water (app. 2.5 %).

Name: *Mastacembelus erythrotaenia*
Family: Mastacembelidae.
Trade name: Fire eel.
Range: Southeast Asia.
Temp: 24-28°C.   **Max.Size**: 100 cm.
Water: pH 6-8.   **Aquarium**: 200 cm.
Difficulty: 4.
Comments: Carnivorous (piscivorous). Eats small fishes. Live foods. Solitary. Crepuscular and nocturnal. Brackish water (app.1%). Very sensitive. Needs fine sand, floating plants and, several hiding-places.

171

Mark Smith

Mark Smith

Name: *Monocirrhus polyacanthus*
Family: Nandidae.
Trade name: Leaf fish.
Range: Guyana to Brazil.
Temp: 24-26°C.   **Max.Size**: 8 cm.
Water: pH 5-6.5.   **Aquarium**: 100 cm.
Difficulty: 4.
Comments: Carnivorous (piscivorous).
Eats fishes, ambush predator. Live foods only, very greedy. Substrate (leaves, stones) brooder. Needs dense planting, an open swimming area, and several hiding-places (roots, large plants).

Name: *Monodactylus argenteus*
Family: Monodactylidae.
Trade name: Finger fish, Mono, Malayan angel.
Range: Indo-west Pacific.
Temp: 24-27°C.   **Max.Size**: 25 cm.
Water: pH 7-8.   **Aquarium**: 120 cm.
Difficulty: 4.
Comments: Omnivorous. Eats small fishes. Eats all normal foods. Peaceful. Shoaling fish, but somewhat shy. Only in marine or brackish water.

Mark Smith

Mark Smith

Name: *Oryzias melastigmus*
Family: Adrianichthyidae.
Trade name: Oryzias javanicus, Javan medaka.
Range: Tropical Asia.
Temp: 22-26°C.   **Max.Size**: 7 cm.
Water: pH 6-7.5.   **Aquarium**: 80 cm.
Difficulty: 2.
Comments: Carnivorous and omnivorous. Eats all normal foods. Substrate (plants) spawner. Rather peaceful. Needs fine sand, dense planting, floating plants, and an open swimming area.

Name: *Osteoglossum bicirrhosum*
Family: Osteoglossidae.
Trade name: Arowana.
Range: Amazon river system.
Temp: 24-28°C.   **Max.Size**: 120 cm.
Water: pH 6-7.   **Aquarium**: 300 cm.
Difficulty: 4.
Comments: Carnivorous (piscivorous).
Eats fishes and all normal foods. Keep only with very big fishes. Aggressive towards its own kind. Mouth brooder. Grows fast. Jumps. Juveniles (up to two years) in a 200 cm aquarium.

Name: *Osteoglossum ferreirai* (juvenile)
Family: Osteoglossidae.
Trade name: Black arowana.
Range: Amazon basin.
Temp: 24-28°C. **Max.Size**: 100 cm.
Water: pH 6-7. **Aquarium**: 300 cm.
Difficulty: 4.
Comments: Carnivorous (piscivorous).
Eats fishes and all normal foods. Keep
only with very big fishes. Aggressive to-
wards its own kind. Mouth brooder. Grows
fast. Jumps. Juveniles (up to two years)
in a 200 cm aquarium.

Name: *Pantodon buchholzi*
Family: Pantodontidae.
Trade name: Butterflyfish.
Range: Nigeria, Cameroon, Zaire.
Temp: 25-28°C. **Max.Size**: 10 cm.
Water: pH 6-7. **Aquarium**: 100 cm.
Difficulty: 3.
Comments: Carnivorous (piscivorous).
Eats small fishes. Needs live foods, but
accepts dry food. Egg scatterer. Surface
swimmer. Needs floating plants. Jumps.

Name: *Papyrocranus afer*
Family: Notopteridae.
Trade name: Reticulate knifefish.
Range: West Africa.
Temp: 23-28°C. **Max.Size**: 80 cm.
Water: pH 6-7. **Aquarium**: 200 cm.
Difficulty: 4.
Comments: Carnivorous. Live foods, in-
cluding fishes. Crepuscular and noctur-
nal. Mouth brooder. Aggressive towards
its own kind. Needs dense planting, an
open swimming area, floating plants, and
hiding-places.

Name: *Parambassis ranga*
Family: Ambassidae.
Trade name: *Chanda ranga*, Indian
glassfish.
Range: Tropical Asia.
Temp: 22-28°C. **Max.Size**: 8 cm.
Water: pH 7-8 **Aquarium**: 80 cm.
Difficulty: 3 **Comments**: Carni-
vorous. Eats all normal foods. Peaceful.
Shoaling fish. Sometimes imported from
Asia, injected with dye — avoid such
stock, do not encourage cruelty. Needs
dense planting and hiding-places.

173

Name: *Periophthalmus barbarus*
Family: Gobiidae.
Trade name: Mudskipper.
Range: Mangrove swamps, around the world.
Temp: 25-29°C.   **Max.Size**: 25 cm.
Water: pH 7.5-8.5. **Aquarium**: 150 cm.
Difficulty: 3.
Comments: Carnivorous. Eats all normal foods, but prefers live foods. Amphibious can breathe air. Territorial. Needs fine sand, large bottom area and a emerse "bank" area. Sensitive. Territorial. Brackish water.

Name: *Polycentrus schomburgki*
Family: Nandidae.
Trade name: *Polycentrus punctatus*, Schomburgk´s leaf fish.
Range: Central America, Northeastern South America.
Temp: 22-26°C.   **Max.Size**: 10 cm.
Water: pH 6-7.   **Aquarium**: 100 cm.
Difficulty: 3.
Comments: Piscivorous. Eats small fishes. Live foods. Substrate (cave or leaf) brooder. Crepuscular and nocturnal. Solitary. Shy. Needs fine sand and several hiding-places. Accepts brackish waters.

Name: *Polypterus delhezi*
Family: Polypteridae.
Trade name: Barred bichir.
Range: Congo river basin.
Temp: 24-28°C.   **Max.Size**: 35 cm.
Water: pH 6.5-7.5. **Aquarium**: 120 cm.
Difficulty: 3.
Comments: Carnivorous (piscivorous). Eats fishes. Live foods. Egg scatterer. Aggressive towards its own kind. Needs shallow water, an open swimming area, and several hiding-places.

Name: *Polypterus retropinnis*
Family: Polypteridae.
Trade name: West African bichir.
Range: Liberia to Cameroon, Central Congo River Basin and Ogoué River.
Temp: 24-28°C.   **Max.Size**: 33 cm.
Water: pH 6.5-7.5. **Aquarium**: 150 cm.
Difficulty: 4.
Comments: Carnivorous (piscivorous). Eats fishes. Live foods. Egg scatterer. Aggressive towards its own kind. Needs an open swimming area, and several hiding-places.

Name: *Potamotrygon laticeps*
Family: Potamotrygonidae.
Trade name: *S*tingray.
Range: Tropical South America.
Temp: 23-26°C.   **Max.Size**: 60 cm.
Water: pH 6.5-7.   **Aquarium**: 200 cm.
Difficulty: 4.
Comments: Carnivorous. Live and frozen foods. Peaceful but can eat small bottom-dwelling fishes. Live bearer. Aquariums with large bottom area with fine sand (max. 2 mm). Sensitive. Watch out for the poisonous spines.

Name: *Protopterus annectens annectens*
Family: Protopteridae.
Trade name: African lungfish.
Range: From Senegal to Nigeria.
Temp: 25-30°C.   **Max.Size**: 100 cm.
Water: pH 6.5-7.5. **Aquarium**: 200 cm.
Difficulty: 4.
Comments: Carnivorous. Piscivorous. Live foods, e.g. fishes. Air breather. Aggressive. Substrate brooder. Only young specimens are suitable for the aquarium. Can survive six months in the mud in the dry season. Jumps.

Name: *Scatophagus argus*
Family: Scatophagidae.
Trade name: Argusfish, Scat.
Range: Tropical Indo-Pacific.
Temp: 20-26°C.   **Max.Size**: 35 cm.
Water: pH 7-8.5.   **Aquarium**: 130 cm.
Difficulty: 4.
Comments: Omnivorous. Eats all normal foods, including plants. Peaceful. Shoaling fishes. Brackish water (0.5%). Adult specimens need more salt in the water. Needs hiding-places and some plants.

Name: *Scatophagus multifasciatus*
Family: Scatophagidae.
Trade name: *Selenotoca multifasciata*.
Range: Papua New Guinea to Australia.
Temp: 22-28°C.   **Max.Size**: 45 cm.
Water: pH 7-8.5.   **Aquarium**: 200 cm.
Difficulty: 4.
Comments: Omnivorous and herbivorous. Eats all normal foods, including plants. Peaceful. Shoaling fish. Brackish water (0.5%). Adult specimens need more salt in the water.

Name: *Scleropages formosus*
Family: Osteoglossidae.
Trade name: Asian arowana.
Range: Southeast Asia.
Temp: 23-28°C.   **Max.Size**: 100 cm.
Water: pH 7-8.   **Aquarium**: 300 cm.
Difficulty: 4.
Comments: See Osteoglossum for information. Popular aquarium fish in Asia and bred in several colour-variants. This fish is protected (Cites listed), therefore occurs only bred fishes in the trade.

Name: *Syngnathus abaster*
Family: Syngnathidae.
Trade name: *Syngnathus nigrolineatus*, pipefish.
Range: Europe and Asia.
Temp: 10-26°C.   **Max.Size**: 21 cm.
Water: pH 7-8.   **Aquarium**: 130 cm.
Difficulty: 4.
Comments: Carnivorous. Eats only live foods. Peaceful. Marine or rock salt in the water (0.1%). Needs dense planting and hiding-places.

Name: *Tetraodon fluviatilis*
Family: Tetraodontidae.
Trade name: Green puffer.
Range: Tropical Asia.
Temp: 23-27°C.   **Max.Size**: 15 cm.
Water: pH 7-8.   **Aquarium**: 100 cm.
Difficulty: 4.
Comments: Carnivorous. Live foods; eat snails and vegetable foods. Substrate brooder. Adults are very aggressive. Solitary. Needs several hiding-places. Can live in freshwater, but prefers brackish water.

Name: *Tetraodon mbu*
Family: Tetraodontidae.
Trade name: Giant puffer, Mbu puffer.
Range: East and West Africa.
Temp: 23-26°C.   **Max.Size**: 65 cm.
Water: pH 6.5-7.5. **Aquarium**: 250 cm.
Difficulty: 5.
Comments: Carnivorous. Live foods, snails, and shell fish. Young fishes peaceful. Adult are extremely aggressive. Solitary. Needs several hiding-places. Too big for most aquaria.

Name: *Tetraodon miurus*
Family: Tetraodontiae.
Trade name: Congo puffer.
Range: Congo basin.
Temp: 23-28°C.   **Max.Size**: 15 cm.
Water: pH 6.5-7.5. **Aquarium**: 120 cm.
Difficulty: 4.
Comments: Carnivorous (piscivorous).
Eats smaller fishes. Live foods. Young
fishes are rather peaceful. Adults are very
aggressive. Solitary. Needs fine sand and
several hiding-places.

Name: *Toxotes jaculator*
Family: Toxotidae.
Trade name: *T. jaculatrix*, Archerfish.
Range: Southern Asia and Oceania.
Temp: 25-30°C.   **Max.Size**: 30 cm.
Water: pH 7-8.   **Aquarium**: 120 cm.
Difficulty: 4.   **Comments**: Carnivorous. Live foods. Prefers insects on the
waters surface. Can shoot down insects,
with a jet of water, up to 150 cm above
the waters surface. Peaceful, but older
specimens can be aggressive. Shoaling
fish.

Name: *Xenentodon cancila*
Family: Belonidae.
Trade name: Freshwater garfish.
Range: Tropical Asia.
Temp: 23-26°C.   **Max.Size**: 40 cm.
Water: pH 7-7.5.   **Aquarium**: 200 cm.
Difficulty: 5.
Comments: Carnivorous (piscivorous).
Live foods, but also frozen foods. Do not
keep with smaller fishes. Shoaling fish.
Needs fine sand and an open swimming
area. Jumps.

Name: *Xenomystus nigri*
Family: Notopteridae.
Trade name: African knifefish.
Range: West Africa.
Temp: 23-26°C.   **Max.Size**: 20 cm.
Water: pH 6-7.5.   **Aquarium**: 120 cm.
Difficulty: 3.
Comments: Carnivorous. Live and frozen
foods. Young specimens are shoaling
fishes. Older fishes are solitary. Crepus-
cular and nocturnal. Needs hiding-places.

177

Plants

When you buy plants for your aquarium you must consider how the different plants will fit together and whether they have the same requirements as regards pH and temperature. On the other hand the light requirement is not so important since it is possible to site the plants at different places in the aquarium, at different distances from the light source. By the time you buy your plants you should have a plan of where in the aquarium each plant is to be sited. We often talk about background and foreground plants. Examples of good background plants are some species of the genera *Crinum, Sagittaria, Echinodorus, Vallisneria*, and *Hygrophila*. These plants have in common the fact that they grow fairly tall, and be-

cause of this they are excellent plants for siting in the back part of the aquarium as well as near the ends. Some example of good plants for the foreground and middle part of the aquarium (foreground plants) are some species of the genera *Anubias, Cryptocoryne, Echinodorus*, and *Eleocharis*. But note that these genera also include some species that grow tall (more than 30 cm). So check with the information about each plant on the following pages.

As mentioned earlier in the book (see DECOR) it is easier to decorate the aquarium with plants if the layer of gravel is deeper at the back of the aquarium and slopes downwards towards the front glass. In order to make the gravel more stable you can build some

Ulle Pedersen

terraces with the help of stones and wood. Nowadays there are also plants available in the trade that are sold ready-attached to a piece of wood or stone. Including a few pieces of wood and rock in the decor of a planted aquarium makes it more attractive.

Introduction to plant section

On the following pages we briefly introduce the most common aquarium plants. The list is far from complete and includes only those plants that are most commonly found in aquarium shops. Aquarists especially interested in plants and planted aquariums are recommended to read a book on this specialised subject.

The following is a brief explanation of the text that accompanies each photo.

Name: The scientific name or the trade name.

Family: The plant family to which it belongs.

Origin: From which part of the world or which country the plant originates.

Height: The height of the plant in the aquarium after approximately 2 months under the correct conditions. The lower number stands for the growth with minimum "light requirements", the higher number for the growth with maximum "light requirements".

Light requirements: On a scale of 1 to 5: 1 = very small light requirement; 2 = small light requirement 3 = normal requirement; 4 = high light requirement; 5 = very high light requirement. Two numbers are mentioned. The lower is the minimum light requirements. The higher is the maximum light requirements.

Temperature: Suitable temperature range. The optimum temperature is that at the middle of the range.

Water: The pH level of the water (see WATER page 16).

Growth: On a scale of 1-5: 1 = grows very slowly; 2 = grows slowly; 3 = average; 4 = grows fast; 5 = grows very fast.

Difficulty: On a scale of 1-5: 1 = Very easy. Grows very well in all types of aquaria. Extremely hardy. 2 = Easy. Thrives and grows well in most aquaria. 3 = Average. Thrives if conditions are correct. 4 = Difficult. High demands as regards conditions (e.g. plenty of light) required in order to thrive. 5 = Very difficult. Extremely high requirements as regards, for example, light and/or water conditions.

Comments: In some cases a short comment on the plant is given.

Ole Pedersen

Ole Pedersen

Kjell Fohrman

Name: *Alternanthera reineckii* "lilacina"
Family: Amaranthaceae
Origin: South America.
Height: 15-40 cm.
Light: 4-5.
Temp: 17-28°C.
Water: pH 5-7.
Growth: 2.   **Difficulty**: 4.
Comments: Plant in groups. Needs CO_2.

Name: *Anubias barteri* var. *barteri*
Family: Araceae.
Origin: West Africa.
Height: 25-40 cm.
Light: 1-3.
Temp: 20-30°C.
Water: pH 5.5-9.
Growth: 1.   **Difficulty**: 1.
Comments: Plant on a shady place, to avoid algae on the leaves.

Name: *Anubias barteri* var. *nana*
Family: Araceae.
Origin: Cameron.
Height: 5-15 cm.
Light: 1-3.
Temp: 20-30°C.
Water: pH 5.5-9.
Growth: 1.   **Difficulty**: 1.
Comments: Plant on a shady place, to avoid algae on the leaves.

Ole Pedersen

Jouni Jaakkola

Ole Pedersen

Name: *Aponogeton boivinianus*
Family: Aponogetonaceae.
Origin: Madagascar.
Height: 30-70 cm.
Light: 3-5.
Temp: 16-26°C.
Water: pH 6-8.
Growth: 4.   **Difficulty**: 4.
Comments: Only in large aquaria. Needs period of rest.

Name: *Aponogeton ulvaceus*
Family: Aponogetonaceae.
Origin: Madagascar.
Height: 30-60 cm.
Light: 3-5.
Temp: 20-27°C.
Water: pH 5.5-8.
Growth: 4.   **Difficulty**: 3.
Comments: Only in large aquaria. Needs period of rest.

Name: *Bacopa caroliniana*
Family: Scrophulariaceae.
Origin: USA.
Height: 30-50 cm.
Light: 3-5.
Temp: 15-28°C.
Water: pH 5-8.
Growth: 2.   **Difficulty**: 3.
Comments: Plant in groups.

Ole Pedersen

Ole Pedersen

Ole Pedersen

Name: *Barclaya longifolia*
Family: Nymphaeceae.
Origin: Southeast Asia.
Height: 30-80 cm.
Light: 3-5.
Temp: 23-32°C.
Water: pH 5-8.
Growth: 3.   **Difficulty**: 3.
Comments: Different colour variants exists.

Name: *Blyxa aubertii*
Family: Hydrocharitaceae.
Origin: Asia.
Height: 10-15 cm.
Light: 3-5.
Temp: 22-28°C.
Water: pH 5.5-7.5.
Growth: 3.   **Difficulty**: 4.
Comments: Plant in groups. CO2 and soft water necessary.

Name: *Bolbitis heudelotii*
Family: Lomariopsidaceae.
Origin: West Africa.
Height: 15-40 cm.
Light: 1-4.
Temp: 20-28°C.
Water: pH 5-7.
Growth: 2.   **Difficulty**: 4.
Comments: Best planted on a root or a stone. Best in soft and somewhat acid water.

Kjell Fohrman

Jouni Jaakkola

Ole Pedersen

Name: *Cabomba aquatica*
Family: Cabombaceae.
Origin: America.
Height: 30-70 cm.
Light: 3-5.
Temp: 24-30°C.
Water: pH 5-7.
Growth: 4.   **Difficulty**: 4.
Comments: Needs very strong light and clear water.

Name: *Cardamine lyrata*
Family: Brassicaceae.
Origin: Japan.
Height: 20-50 cm.
Light: 3-5.
Temp: 15-24°C.
Water: pH 6-8.
Growth: 4.   **Difficulty**: 2.
Comments: Plant in groups.

Name: *Ceratophyllum demersum*
Family: Ceratophyllaceae.
Origin: Everywhere.
Height: 5-100 cm.
Light: 1-5.   **Temp:** 10-28°C
Water: pH 6-9.
Growth: 4.   **Difficulty**: 1.
Comments: Offers hiding places for juveniles. Grows fast impeding growth of algae.

Name: *Ceratopteris cornuta*
Family: Pteridaceae.
Origin: Tropical zone.
Height: 25-50 cm.
Light: 3-5.
Temp: 15-28°C.
Water: pH 5-8.5.
Growth: 4.   **Difficulty**: 2.
Comments: Both a floating plant and an underwater plant. Grows fast which will impede growth of algae.

Name: *Crinum thaianum*
Family: Amaryllidaceae.
Origin: Thailand.
Height: 10-30 cm.
Light: 3-5.
Temp: 20-28°C.
Water: pH 5.5-9.
Growth: 3.   **Difficulty**: 2.
Comments: Bulbous plant. When planted 2/3 of the bulb must be seen above the gravel.

Name: *Cryptocoryne crispatula* var. *balansae*
Family: Araceae.
Origin: Thailand.
Height: 20-70 cm.
Light: 2-5.
Temp: 20-28°C.
Water: pH 5-9.
Growth: 3.   **Difficulty**: 2.
Comments: Needs to be acclimatized before it starts to grow.

Name: *Cryptocoryne wendtii* "Brown"
Family: Araceae.
Origin: Sri Lanka.
Height: 15-25 cm.
Light: 2-4.
Temp: 20-30°C.
Water: pH 5.5-9.
Growth: 3.   **Difficulty**: 2.
Comments: Grows rather good in all types of water.

Name: *Dracaena sanderiana*
Family: Araceae.
Origin: Bolivia.
Height: 20-30 cm.
Light: 3-5.
Temp: 20-28°C.
Water: pH 6-8.
Growth: 1.   **Difficulty**: 5.
Comments: Not an aquarium plant. Will survive a few months in the aquarium.

Name: *Echinodorus bleheri*
Family: Alismataceae.
Origin: South America.
Height: 20-50 cm.
Light: 1-5.
Temp: 20-30°C.
Water: pH 5.5-9.
Growth: 4.   **Difficulty**: 2.
Comments: Very popular aquarium plant. Grows better with fertiliser in the gravel.

Ole Pedersen

Ole Pedersen

Kjell Fohrman

Name: *Echinodorus* "Ozelot"
Family: Alismataceae.
Origin: Don't exist in nature.
Height: 20-50 cm.
Light: 2-5.
Temp: 15-30°C.
Water: pH 6-9.
Growth: 4.   **Difficulty**: 2.
Comments: Hybrid between two other *Echinodorus* species.

Name: *Echinodorus tenellus*
Family: Alismataceae.
Origin: America.
Height: 5-10 cm.
Light: 3-5.
Temp: 19-30°C.
Water: pH 5.5-8.
Growth: 3.   **Difficulty**: 3.
Comments: Suitable plant for the foreground. Grows better with fertiliser in the gravel.

Name: *Egeria densa*
Family: Hydrocharitaceae.
Origin: Everythere.
Height: 40-100 cm.
Light: 3-5.
Temp: 10-26°C.
Water: pH 5-10.
Growth: 5.   **Difficulty**: 2.
Comments: Grows fast which will impede growth of algae.

Jouni Jaakkola

Ole Pedersen

Ole Pedersen

Name: *Eustralis stellata*
Family: Lamiaceae.
Origin: Asia.
Height: 15-25 cm.
Light: 4-5.
Temp: 22-28°C.
Water: pH 5-7.
Growth: 3.   **Difficulty**: 5.
Comments: A lot of light and CO2 necessary.

Name: *Glossostigma elatinoides*
Family: Scrophulariaceae.
Origin: New Zealand.
Height: 2-4 cm.   **Light**: 4-5.
Temp: 15-26°C.
Water: pH 5-7.5.
Growth: 4.   **Difficulty**: 5.
Comments: A lot of light and CO2 is necessary. Useful plant for the foreground.

Name: *Hemigraphis colorata*
Family: Acanthaceae.
Origin: Southeast Asia.
Height: 12-25 cm.
Light: 3
Temp: 18-28°C.
Water: pH 6-8.
Growth: 2-4. **Difficulty**: 5.
Comments: Not an aquarium plant. Will survive a few months in the aquarium.

183

Ole Pedersen

Ole Pedersen

Ole Pedersen

Name: *Heteranthera zosterifolia*
Family: Pontederiaceae.
Origin: South America.
Height: 10-15 cm.
Light: 3-5.
Temp: 18-30°C.
Water: pH 5.5-8.
Growth: 4.   **Difficulty**: 2.
Comments: Very hardy plant if there is enough light.

Name: *Hydrocotyle leucocephala*
Family: Apiaceae.
Origin: South America.
Height: 10-20 cm.
Light: 2-5.
Temp: 15-28°C.
Water: pH 5-9.
Growth: 4.   **Difficulty**: 2.
Comments: Can be planted, but also used as a floating plant.

Name: *Hygrophila corymbosa* "Siamensis"
Family: Acanthaceae.
Origin: Southeast Asia.
Height: 15-40 cm.
Light: 2-5.
Temp: 20-28°C.
Water: pH 5.5-8.
Growth: 4.   **Difficulty**: 2.
Comments: Can grow up above the water level.

Ole Pedersen

Kjell Fohrman

Ole Pedersen

Name: *Hygrophila difformis*
Family: Acanthaceae.
Origin: Southeast Asia.
Height: 20-50 cm.
Light: 3-5.
Temp: 22-30°C.
Water: pH 5-9.
Growth: 4.   **Difficulty**: 2.
Comments: Suitable plant to start with. Grows fast which will impede growth of algae.

Name: *Hygrophila polysperma*
Family: Acanthaceae.
Origin: Southeast Asia.
Height: 25-40 cm.
Light: 2-5.
Temp: 18-30°C.
Water: pH 5-9.
Growth: 5.   **Difficulty**: 1.
Comments: One of the best plants to start with. Good against algae.

Name: *Lilaeopsis brasiliensis*
Family: Apiaceae.
Origin: South America.
Height: 4-7 cm.
Light: 4-5.
Temp: 15-26°C.
Water: pH 6-8.
Growth: 2.   **Difficulty**: 4.
Comments: Needs very strong light. Can live in brackish water.

Ole Pedersen

Ole Pedersen

Ole Pedersen

Name: *Limnophila sessiliflora*
Family: Scrophulariaceae.
Origin: Southeast Asia.
Height: 15-40 cm.
Light: 3-5.
Temp: 20-30°C.
Water: pH 5-8.
Growth: 4.   **Difficulty**: 3.
Comments: Plant in groups. Needs CO2. Reminds of *Cabomba*, but doesn't demand so much light.

Name: *Microsorum pteropus*
Family: Polypodiaeceae.
Origin: Southeast Asia.
Height: 15-30 cm.
Light: 1-4.
Temp: 18-30°C.
Water: pH 5-8.
Growth: 2.   **Difficulty**: 1.
Comments: Should be planted on a stone or a root. Accepts brackish water.

Name: *Microsorum pteropus* "Windeløv"
Family: Polypodiaeceae.
Origin: Don't exist in nature.
Height: 10-20 cm.
Light: 1-4.
Temp: 18-30°C
Water: pH 5-8.
Growth: 2.   **Difficulty**: 1.
Comments: Bred variant of *M. pteropus*. Should be planted on a stone or a root.

Jouni Jaakkola

Ole Pedersen

Ole Pedersen

Name: *Myriophyllum aquaticum*
Family: Haloragaceae.
Origin: South America.
Height: 40-60 cm.
Light: 4   **Temp**: 18-29°C
Water: pH 5.5-9.
Growth: 4-5. **Difficulty**: 4.
Comments: Needs strong light, CO2 and fertiliser. Plant in groups.

Name: *Myriophyllum tuberculatum*
Family: Haloragaceae.
Origin: South America.
Height: 40-60 cm.
Light: 5.   **Temp**: 18-29°C
Water: pH 5-7.
Growth: 4.   **Difficulty**: 5.
Comments: Needs strong light, CO2 and fertiliser. Plant in groups.

Name: *Pistia stratiotes*
Family: Araceae.
Origin: Tropical zone.
Height: 5-25 cm.
Light: 4-5.
Temp: 17-30°C.
Water: pH 5-8.
Growth: 4.   **Difficulty**: 3.
Comments: Useful floating plant.

185

Ole Pedersen

Ole Pedersen

Ole Pedersen

Name: *Riccia fluitans*
Family: Ricciaceae.
Origin: Everywhere.
Height: 0.5-1.5 cm.
Light: 2-5.
Temp: 10-28°C.
Water: pH 5-8.
Growth: 3.   **Difficulty**: 3.
Comments: Plant on stones. Needs CO2.

Name: *Rotala* sp. "Nanjens-han"
Family: Lythraceae.
Origin: Southeast Asia
Height: 10-15 cm.
Light: 4-5.
Temp: 20-30°C.
Water: pH 5.5-8.
Growth: 4.   **Difficulty**: 3.
Comments: Plant in groups. Needs CO2.

Name: *Sagittaria subulata*
Family: Alismataceae.
Origin: America
Height: 5-35 cm.
Light: 2-5.
Temp: 16-28°C.
Water: pH 6-9.
Growth: 4.   **Difficulty**: 2.
Comments: Suitable foreground plant, but may sometimes grow up to 50 cm.

Kjell Fohrman

Ole Pedersen

Ole Pedersen

Name: *Spathiphyllum wallisii*
Family: Araceae.
Origin: South America
Height: 15-25 cm.
Light: 2-4.
Temp: 22-25°C.
Water: pH 5-7.
Growth: 1.   **Difficulty**: 5.
Comments: Not an aquarium plant. Will survive a few months in the aquarium.

Name: *Vallisneria americana* var. *biwaensis*
Family: Hydrocharitaceae.
Origin: Southeast Asia
Height: 20-80 cm.
Light: 3-5.   **Temp:** 20-28°C
Water: pH 6-8.5.
Growth: 3.   **Difficulty**: 3.
Comments: Vallisneria sp. are popular aquarium plants, especially in cichlid aquaria.

Name: *Vesicularia dubyana*
Family: Hydrocharitaceae.
Origin: Southeast Asia
Height: 20-80 cm.
Light: 1-5.   **Temp:** 20-28°C
Water: pH 6-8.5.
Growth: 3.   **Difficulty**: 3.
Comments: Called Java moss. Offers hiding places for juveniles. Best planted on a stone or a root.

Literature

The Back to Nature Aquarium guide is a general introduction to the aquarium hobby. If you wish to specialise in a particular group of aquarium fishes, or are an experienced aquarist who wants to learn more, then this book is probably not what you are looking for — instead I suggest you read other books intended for more advanced/specialised hobbyists, take out a subscription to an aquarium magazine, or maybe join an aquarium club.

Below are a few examples of books from which you can learn more.

The following books have been published in the Back to Nature series. All are 128 pages long and contain approximately 300 colour photos apiece.

Back to Nature guide to Tanganyika cichlids. Ad Konings (now out of print).
Back to Nature guide to Catfishes. David Sands.
Back to Nature guide to Malawi cichlids. Ad Konings.
Back to Nature guide to Discus. Dick Au.

Cichlid Press (USA) specialises in cichlid-related books. You will find full information about books from this publisher at www. cichlidpress.com.

Verlag A.C.S in Germany publishes the "Aqualog" series, bilingual (German/English) photographic lexicons of various fish groups, as well as the "Aqualog Special" textbooks (again on specific groups). You will find information about the books from this publisher on www.aqualog.de.

Mergus Verlag in Germany have published a series of Aquarium Atlases, whose author is Hans A. Baensch. Several thousand fishes are included in these books.

Aquadocumenta Verlag in Germany has published "My first Aquarium" by Kaspar Horst. This book is for beginners.

When I wrote this book I found a lot of relevant information on the Internet, mainly on the "Fishbase" website: www.cqiar.org/clarm/fishbase/search.cfm.

Index

188

189

190